Cacti and their cultivation

CACTI
and their cultivation

Margaret J. Martin
P. R. Chapman
H. A. Auger

CHARLES SCRIBNER'S SONS
New York

3 5 7 9 11 13 15 17 19 M/P 20 18 16 14 12 10 8 6 4 2

Printed in the United States of America
Library of Congress Catalog Card Number 75-165330
ISBN O-684-14365-8

CONTENTS

ILLUSTRATIONS

Illustrations

Illustrations

MAPS

9

ACKNOWLEDGEMENTS

We should like to express our grateful thanks to Mr G. D. Rowley, of the Department of Botany of Reading University, for reading the manuscript and offering suggestions, and also to Mr E. W. Putnam of the Succulent Plant Institute, for reading and commenting on the section on *Gymnocalycium*. The habitat photograph of *Carnegiea gigantea* was kindly supplied by Mr C. P. R. Cummins. All the other photographs were taken by Margaret J. Martin and P. R. Chapman. The material on outdoor landscaping and on specific points related to cactus growing in the United States was supplied by Mrs R. W. Kane.

The United States, Central America and the Caribbean

South America

INTRODUCTION

Growers of more orthodox plants may well consider cactus enthusiasts to be rather odd, since there are probably more misconceptions about these plants than any others. One has only to listen to comments made by visitors to a botanical gardens' collection to realise that, to many people, cacti are 'a race apart'.

However, the purpose of this book is not so much to stimulate an interest in cacti as to develop an already existing one, since there are many small popular books on the market designed to cater for the absolute beginner, who may not be quite sure whether he wants to collect cacti or not. A cactus collection may have quite small beginnings, possibly a few cuttings given by a friend, as a novelty, or a small plant bought from a florist. In the case of one of the authors, the interest developed from a packet of cactus seed purchased from a chain store. The few plants thus acquired may eventually pass away through ignorance or neglect; the incipient collector may decide that they are not really worth bothering about, and his interest will die also. On the other hand, he may feel his interest growing, and whether his first plants survive or not, he will have the urge to continue. At this stage he will usually try to find out more about these strange plants and probably either discuss them with more experienced friends, or purchase one of the many small books on cacti. By this time he will have been firmly 'hooked' by this fascinating hobby and his available window space will be rapidly filling; he may even consider a greenhouse for his expanding collection. Useful as he may have found his simple book, he will now most probably wish to carry his reading a stage further in order to find out more about the plants, and cacti in general. This is where we hope our book will be found profitable. Although the absolute beginner can certainly use it, it is designed mainly for those who require more information and help than the low-priced books can give, excellent as they mostly are, as far as they go. For readers who wish to study the *Cactaceae* in more detail than we can give in a book of this size, we have listed some of the standard works on this family in the Appendix. Some of these consist of several volumes, are very expensive, and are suitable as references for the real specialist.

About 2,000 species of cacti are recognised, included in about 200 genera, so that, although we should have liked to describe every plant that the collector may meet, this is obviously impossible. Omissions are particularly noticeable in the case of *Mammillaria* where we have only been able to mention a relatively small number of the many plants in cultivation. Whole books have been written on this genus.

The authors have been collecting and growing cacti and other succulent plants for many years, and this book is based largely upon practical experience. The various methods of cultivation we have described are those that we have found satisfactory, but as is usual in horticultural matters, it is impossible to be dogmatic. Books are to be used as a guidance, certainly as far as cultivation is concerned, as differing conditions may cause differing treatment to be needed. Cultivation is basically a matter of common sense, and consideration of the natural habitat of the plants will help.

Some genera of cacti, for example *Notocactus* and *Neoporteria*, are receiving considerable attention from the taxonomists and this has resulted in confusion of nomenclature. We have attempted to name the plants in accordance with the most recent ideas, but future changes may make these out of date in a relatively short time. However, the average grower will probably not bother too much about this, and the book is not in any case designed for taxonomists.

Units of size and weight have been given both in metric and standard measure.

Certain cacti have been grouped together for convenience, because of particular characteristics in common; the rest are included in the chapters on North and South America, although all the plants do in fact come from these regions.

ONE

What is a Cactus?

A cactus collector is scarcely different from a collector of porcelain or other choice objects; if he sees a shop stocking the appropriate goods (in our case a florist), he has to go and have a look round inside. There may be a rarity waiting to be picked up. He is often disappointed. A florist may have a tray of plants labelled cacti without there being a cactus amongst the lot. All fat prickly plants are not cacti, neither are all cacti rotund and leafless.

Cacti are members of the *Cactaceae* family; they have a number of characteristics which distinguish them from the members of other plant families. The most obvious one is the areole. This is a small, cushion-like structure found on the stems, from which grow the spines, leaves and flowers. Even out of flower a cactus can be definitely identified by the presence of this areole. The large columnar euphorbias bear a strong resemblance to the tall-growing cerei, but on taking a closer look at the plants, it is very easy to pick out the cactus from the euphorbia. The euphorbia spines do not come from areoles. These cerei and euphorbias are an example of parallel evolution.

The majority of cacti are succulent plants, the exceptions being pereskias which are only slightly fleshy. These are leafy shrubs or climbers found in the tropical regions of America. The two things which distinguish pereskias from the numerous other straggly shrubs found around the world are the areoles on the stems and the typical cactus flowers. Before giving a detailed description of a cactus, we will explain the term 'succulent plant'.

There are perhaps 10,000 plants, in many different families, which qualify for the title of 'succulent', this term being applied to plants which have developed water storage cells in their leaves, stems or roots. This storage tissue enables them to survive periods of drought by living on stored water, rather like the camel. Like the camel, at the end of their abstinence, they are thin and shrivelled. The rains come and the plants absorb water, plumping up overnight. They grow and flower during the wet season, and store up more water for the coming dry months.

Succulents can be roughly divided into two classes; leaf succulents and stem succulents. The cacti belong to the second class. The leaves of the succulent *Cactaceae* have either disappeared completely, or exist as tiny degenerate structures which soon shrivel and fall off. One minor exception to this is the more persistent leaf system of some of the cylindrical opuntias, but even here the leaf area is far less than that of the stem, and plays only a minor role in photosynthesis. In all cases, photosynthesis has been taken over by the stem. This is common to all stem succulents whether cacti or euphorbias.

The stem of this type of succulent contains chlorophyll, and is very much thickened due to the presence of large water storage cells, which form a sponge-like tissue inside the body of the plant. The stem is frequently covered with wax, meal, or hair, all of which cut down the evaporation of water. The plants from very arid regions are often spherical. The sphere is the shape with the smallest surface area in relation to its volume, and is the ideal one for a plant which needs to have the minimum evaporating surface. A well-constructed succulent plant can withstand months without water, often under a very hot sun.

Having described in general terms a stem succulent, we can look at a cactus in detail, remembering that whilst most cacti are succulent, by no means are all succulents cacti. A plant can be divided into two parts, the root which is below ground and the shoot which is the part we see.

Plant collectors often include a pick-axe and crowbar amongst their equipment, and for some of the Mexican cacti this may be necessary. Lophophoras and some of the ariocarpus have long taproots which, in many cases go far down into rock crevasses, but the majority of cacti have shallow root systems. The roots spread out for great distances around the plant, 5–10 cm. (2–4 in.) below soil level, enabling the maximum use to be made of the heavy dews. Tall plants with shallow roots are unstable and some of the

What is a Cactus?

immense cerei often fall victims to high winds. Dr W. A. Cannon of the Tucson Desert Laboratory unravelled the root system of a specimen of *Ferocactus wislizenii* and found that the roots were 6 cm. (2½ in.) deep and could be traced for over 3 m. (10 ft.) from the stem. A 120-cm. (4-ft.) *Carnegiea gigantea* investigated by Dr Cannon had its roots about 10 cm. (4 in.) below the surface and extending for about 5 m. (17 ft.) and more.

There are a few cacti which store water in large, tuberous roots. The peniocerei and wilcoxias have turnip-like roots, and specimens of *Peniocereus greggii* have been found with roots weighing 50 kg. (110 lb.), sometimes over this.

Succulent cacti can be roughly divided into two types, the epiphytic, and desert. The epiphytes, found growing on trees in the jungle, have flattened, leaf-like stems with the areoles along the notched edges. Although often called leaves by the uninitiated it is easy to show that this flattened stem is not a leaf since it bears the flowers, which leaves do not. These epiphytes must not be confused with the opuntias, which have flattened stems or 'pads'. The whole surface of the opuntia pad is dotted with areoles.

Desert cacti are more variable in form. They may be columns 12 m. (40 ft.) high, or little spheres less than 2·5 cm. (1 in.) in diameter. Many of these plants have pronounced ribs; this concertina-like structure enables the plant to expand and contract as it gains or loses water, without cracking. Some plants, particularly the mammillarias, are not divided into definite ribs, but are covered with tubercles. The areoles are borne on the edges of the ribs or on the tips of the tubercles.

Not all cacti have spines; some like the lophophoras are spineless. But many are armed with long spines, as stout as nails, a formidable defence against grazing animals. Other cacti have small hooked spines which catch on the coats of animals, thus carrying the plant or a piece of it to new territory. A few species of cacti are covered with long silky hair; these are popularly known as the Old Man cacti. The hair presumably protects the epidermis from the drying effects of wind and sun. *Cephalocereus senilis* and *Oreocereus trollii* are two well-known Old Men. Some cacti produce what are known as glochids; these are quite short, barbed hairs or bristles which occur in groups and which can

19

easily be detached. They are produced mainly by the opuntias, and are on the upper part of the areoles.

The flowers of the *Cactaceae* are usually bell-shaped and are not divided into a definite calyx and corolla. The flowers arise directly from the areoles and have no stalk, or peduncle. For this reason, it is not really possible to use cactus flowers as cut flowers in water. The segments of the perianth may be joined to form a long tube; this is particularly noticeable in the echinopsis where the whole flower may be over 22 cm. (9 in.) long.

Cactus flowers come in all colours except a genuine cornflower blue. As in many other families, there are shades of mauve and violet, but a clear blue is lacking. There are night-flowering cacti *(Selenicereus, Hylocereus,* and *Echinopsis)* having white flowers with a sweet scent of lilies. This attracts the moths which pollinate them.

The size of the flowers varies from under 1 cm. across to well over 15 cm. ($\frac{3}{8}$ in. to 6 in.). The largest ones are found on the night-flowering species and the epiphyllum hybrids.

Most cactus flowers are diurnal and will open only in the sun; if there is a prolonged period of cloudy weather, the buds will abort. The flowers close in the evening, and there are some of our cacti we have never seen with their blooms fully opened. The flowers only last for one or two days in most cases, and if these days are not Saturday and Sunday, you have to hope for better luck next year, unless you work at home or are retired. If, however, you want to be certain of seeing your flowers, try echinopsis. They are fully open by ten o'clock at night and usually last most of the next day. Some of the night-blooming cerei do not open until about midnight and have faded before breakfast time. The epiphyllum are easy to see in bloom as, once the buds are fully formed, they will open without full sun. This they usually do in the evening and they will remain open for a day or so.

The flowers may be followed by seed-pods, which are often brightly coloured. We can only speak from our own experience on the subject of fertility. Some species are always self-fertile; each year most of our *Rebutia, Notocactus, Wigginsia* and *Lophophora williamsii* have seed-pods, although frequently no other species was in bloom at the same time. They ripen and eventually produce seedlings like the parent plant. *Astrophytum myriostigma,*

What is a Cactus?

Gymnocalycium mihanovichii and *Pelecyphora valdezianus* have all set seed once in the many years we have had them. The seed was fertile and there was no possibility of cross-pollination. We have not had seed-pods on *Echinopsis, Lobivia, Parodia* or *Neoporteria* unless deliberately cross-pollinated from another plant. The whole question of self-fertility or sterility in cacti is somewhat involved, and different growers have different opinions on the subject, according to their success or failure. However, if you wish to see seed-pods on your plants, you can always pollinate from one to the other, using a small paint brush, provided that two suitable different plants are in flower together. If a plant is self-sterile, it cannot be pollinated from another specimen originating from the same clone, but a plant coming from the same parent (sibcrossing) can be used. If you pollinate from another species of the same genus, as is the most likely, you will produce hybrids. It is particularly attractive to have seed-pods on mammillarias (many of which will produce them without any aid) as they are mostly of various shades of red, and long-lasting. They also take a long time to form, usually appearing the year after pollination has taken place, so that one year's flowers and the previous year's berries occur on the same plant. When deliberately cross-pollinating, carefully note the parentage; the new seedlings may be more beautiful than their parents, but there is a good chance that they will be less attractive. It is irritating to sow what you think is named seed, and to obtain only a pan of nondescript hybrids. Also, be careful not to give away or otherwise spread around seeds or plants from crosses between different species unless there is a good reason to do so and the recipient is well-warned; the classification of some genera of cacti has been greatly complicated by the indiscriminate production of hybrids, and it is up to all growers not to make the situation even worse.

Some collectors feel very strongly about hybrids. A natural hybrid is fine, but one that originated in a greenhouse is a most sinister plant! Real purists will not cultivate the beautiful epiphyllum hybrids which are so popular both here and in the United States. They are not pure. Our own feeling on the subject is clear; if a plant is beautiful, it is welcome to a space in our greenhouse. We have some beautiful echinopsis which are labelled 'Hybrid white' or 'Hybrid pink'. It may be heresy to say so, but they are

What is a Cactus?

larger and more sweetly scented than some of the named species. However, we do get very annoyed when we buy some expensive named seedling, only to see it grow up into another hybrid white.

HABITAT

Cacti are natives of America. All those 'Prickly Pears' which are such a typical part of the Mediterranean landscape are descended from plants brought from America many years ago. However, there is one genus, *Rhipsalis*, which causes the botanists some embarrassment. *R. erythrocarpa* has been found in East Africa, *R. sansibarica* in Zanzibar, and *R. madagascariensis* in Madagascar, and there is no evidence of them having been imported. To get over these awkward plants, it is assumed that the seeds were dispersed by man or carried by birds; sometimes ocean currents or streams of air are suggested.

It is generally well known that cacti come from deserts, and to some extent this is true. However, the popular idea of a desert is often inaccurate; it is not a sandy waste where it never rains. The word 'desert' comes from the Latin, meaning 'abandoned', but most deserts are by no means devoid of animal and plant life. Those who have learnt to live in and understand the deserts have found them to be fascinating places.

The definition of a desert is based mainly upon the Köppen system for classification of climate, and is characterised by less than 25 cm. (10 in.) annual rainfall and usually high temperatures, but apart from this, the world's deserts are quite varied. Extreme deserts with the lowest rainfall or atmospheric moisture can support little or no life, and plants are not found there. It is not only the low rainfall which determines a desert, but the fact that this rain usually all falls in a very short space of time. For most of the year the desert is certainly a very dry place, but when it does rain it does so with an intensity seldom seen in more temperate climates.

The native cacti of the American continent spread from the tip of South America, up through the United States to British Columbia in western Canada. Many of these plants come from regions of torrential rains. Months of drought are followed by tropical storms, and they may be left standing in mud, or may even be under water for short periods. Other cacti occur in areas where it rarely rains, but have very heavy dews or thick mists, this moisture being enough to keep the plants alive. These latter are amongst the most difficult species to cultivate under our conditions.

Cacti are not solitary plants. Groves of tall cerei grow on the hills of South America, and even such rarities as *Strombocactus disciformis* form large colonies on certain hillsides in Mexico. Cacti are also found growing among xerophytic shrubs and other succulent plants, such as agaves and echeverias.

Many of the smaller cacti, such as rebutias, grow in the grasslands where they obtain some shade from the sun. The shady sides of rocks and boulders also provide congenial homes for cacti, for it must be realised that the intensity of sunlight in their native lands is far greater than we experience in temperate climates.

The epiphytic cacti share their trees with orchids, bromeliads and tropical ferns. These cacti attach themselves to the barks of trees, or grow in pockets of leafmould which form among the twigs and branches. Although they are growing in rain forests, their roots are in very shallow compost, which dries out rapidly. Some germinate in the soil, climb, and later lose contact with the ground.

A few cacti are found in Western Canada where they spend their winters under snow. This is not the slushy snow of England, but the dry, cold climate of Alberta and British Columbia. These can survive many degrees of frost, but not the damp of climates like that of the British Isles and the coast of the American Pacific Northwest, where they need greenhouse protection. Opuntias have been kept outside all the year in some well-drained situations. However, it usually only needs a particularly mild, damp winter to kill them off.

Moving southwards through the western United States, the number of species of cacti increases; oddly, they are scarce in the eastern states of that country. In Texas and Arizona many of the large cacti begin to appear, *Carnegiea gigantea*, the echinocacti and the ferocacti.

Mexico is the home of the mammillarias and the very dry states of northern and central Mexico are the lands where the really

What is a Cactus?

desirable cacti, ariocarpus, pelecyphoras and other choice plants are found. These are often very difficult to locate. The wind blows the dusty soil around and covers everything with a layer of grit, including the plants.

In the southern part of Mexico and Central America tropical forests occur, and here are found the epiphytic cacti: *Hylocereus, Selenicereus* and *Epiphyllum*.

Further south still is the great South American continent; this is the home of many of the most beautiful cacti in cultivation. The small, easily-flowered rebutias, parodias and many others are found here. Also there are tall growing cerei and numerous species of opuntias. West of the Andes the climate is very dry; many of the plants which exist mainly on dew and mists occur in northern Chile. In high altitudes in this region, although near the equator, the climate is of an Alpine type, and here are found the hairy cerei, oreocerei and espostoas in areas of snow and frost. On the eastern side of the Andes conditions are less severe and the grassy plains of Argentina carry a large and varied cactus population. In fact, enormous numbers of the small, easily-flowered plants come from that country; you could have a wonderful collection of flowering cacti if you only grew those from Argentina.

MYTHS

Cacti seem to have attracted to themselves all sorts of queer tales. The most commonly heard one is that they bloom once every seven years. Seven seems to be a 'magic' number amongst the superstitious, but just why it should have attached itself to plants is difficult to say. A mature cactus flowers annually. If it fails to bud up, it has in some way been incorrectly cultivated; this may not always be the fault of the grower since a few plants will not form buds with the lower light intensity of our climate. Alternatively, the plant is immature. Maturity with some species means 12 m. (40 ft.) tall; it would need five times seven before some of the giants flower in nature, let alone in a collection. But once they start to bloom, they continue to do so each year.

Another myth is that cacti grow in sand and need no water, and, judging from some we have seen as desiccated specimens in windows (sometimes florists' windows!), this is quite widely held. As we have said earlier, nothing grows under complete desert conditions. Cacti need water and mineral salts like other plants.

There is even a story abroad that cacti are poisonous. We can assure our readers that a slice of cereus is harmless and has far less taste than a slice of cucumber. If spines are allowed to remain in your finger, they will often fester, but so will any splinter.

Finally we come to a travellers' tale, the story of the thirsty wanderer who beheaded a giant barrel cactus with his hatchet and drank pints of water from inside. But at least one explorer in Mexico (Arthur Douglas) as written that this idea of cactus 'lemonade' is pure fiction. However, in his travels through Mexico, he saw many ferocacti and echinocacti which had been mutilated by the seekers after cactus juice.

USES OF CACTI, PAST AND PRESENT

To the impoverished natives of Mexico and South America the cactus is not just an attractive plant but a source of food and wood. The opuntia supplies not only fruit but also Wopalitos. These are young shoots which are sliced and cooked as a vegetable by the Mexicans. They can be bought bottled in the local shops. The surplus opuntia fruits are dried, like prunes.

Myrtillocactus geometrizans has berries which look like blackcurrants and are sold in the Mexican markets. The fruits of some cerei and epiphyllums are also eaten, and those of various other cacti are candied or otherwise preserved. Some are said to taste like strawberries.

The fruits of the 'saguaro', *Carnegiea gigantea,* the giant cactus of Arizona, are about 8 cm. (3 in.) long, and oval in shape. When ripe they consist of a mass of black seeds in a bright red pulp. This fruit is used by the Indians of the area for making preserves, and even the seeds are ground to make a type of flour.

In California, where the opuntia fruit, or Tuna, are eaten from choice rather than necessity, groves of these cacti are planted for fruit. Some of the Tunas are sold fresh in the local markets whilst the rest are exported in cans for those unfortunates who have no

What is a Cactus?

opuntias growing in their back gardens. Tuna picking must be quite a hazardous occupation.

Even the inhabitants of Northern Europe can benefit from the opuntias. Oil has been extracted from this cactus which is included in a well-known brand of face cream.

Cacti not only provide food; they also provide drink. If 'cactus lemonade' is a myth, cactus wine is a fact. The fruits of cacti are fermented to produce intoxicating liquids, with names like Calonche and Tiswin, which are said to be potent. Unfortunately the writer who described these drinks forgot to mention what they tasted like. We suspect the taste was better forgotten.

In some regions the 'skeletons' of giant cacti are the only readily available source of wood. We say 'skeleton', because these giants are woody and the wood is in the form of a network of fibres inside the fleshy plant body, and not like that of a normal tree. When the plant dies and the fleshy part decays, this fibrous wood remains. The skeleton of *Carnegiea gigantea* has been used for making light furniture, and we have seen most attractive boxes made from cactus wood which are sold to tourists as souvenirs. Dried Cholla (cylindrical opuntia) wood is used by American flower arrangers.

In the past, cactus spines have been used for gramophone needles, and in South America, cereus spines as knitting needles. Before the advent of the aniline dyes, the cochineal insect *(Dactylopius coccus)* was cultivated on opuntias. The dried insect was a source of red dye, being used for the colouring of food and other things.

Finally, we should mention all the nurserymen and explorers who make a living by providing cactus enthusiasts with even more beautiful plants for their greenhouses. There are even people who make money from cacti by writing about them!

NOMENCLATURE

When one first starts collecting cacti, the rather long Latin names seem impossible to remember. After a few months however, names like *Ariocarpus kotschoubeyanus* and *Trichocereus schickendantzii* roll readily off the tongue. Cacti being foreign to this country, they have no popular names. In the United States some

What is a Cactus?

of the nurserymen have invented names for them. Personally we have the same reaction to Angel's Wings and Bunnies' Ears as we have to concrete gnomes—'Ugh!' In any case, popular names can be most confusing, the Purple Flowered Hedgehog of one state is not necessarily the same plant as the Purple Hedgehog of a neighbouring one.

A brief note about botanical names in general may not be out of place here, for those readers who are not familiar with the system. Plants of the same type are grouped together as a 'genus' and given a generic name. Thus we have the groups such as *Opuntia, Mammillaria, Cereus,* etc. Within each group or genus, plants more or less the same, or with only minor differences, are considered to belong to the same species, and we have *Opuntia microdasys, Mammillaria elegans,* or *Cereus peruvianus.* In each case the first name is the generic name and the second the specific epithet. We hope that any botanical readers will excuse this much simplified explanation. Exactly what constitutes a genus and a species in a particular group is sometimes a matter of opinion amongst botanists, and, as we shall see shortly, this causes some confusion.

The very first cacti to be introduced into Europe were the *Melocactus,* only that name came later. They were called *'Cactus',* which also included *Opuntia* and *Cereus.* As more plants were discovered it became necessary to devise more names. Globular plants became *Echinocactus,* and tall ones *Cereus.* It is interesting to look at the index of the book *Cacti* by J. Borg; obsolete names are in italics and current names in normal type. There are seven columns of *Cereus* species and only 26 plants are included in the text under that name. The six columns of *Echinocactus* have been reduced to nine species. No wonder that the genera have proliferated; all these former *Cereus* and *Echinocactus* have to be classified somewhere.

The first important modern classification of the *Cactaceae* was that of Schumann in his published works of 1898–1903, but the standard work on the family is that of Britton and Rose (1919–1923) who divided it into three tribes, the *Pereskieae,* the *Opuntieae* and the *Cereeae.* The *Cereeae,* being a very large tribe, is further divided into eight sub-tribes. These large divisions are made up of smaller groups, the genera, and the genera are divided

27

into species. The above classification is not accepted by all botanists; Buxbaum treats the above tribes as sub-families: *Pereskioideae*, *Opuntioideae*, and *Cereoideae*. The last is split into eight tribes which are again divided into sub-tribes; then come the genera and species. We ourselves are not particularly interested in taxonomy, as this study is called, but for anyone who is, the botanists who have specialised in the *Cactaceae* are Buxbaum and Backeberg on the Continent, the Americans Benson, Hutchinson, Kimnach, Lindsay, Moran, etc., and Donald, Hunt and Rowley in England. Probably we have omitted other important people, but you will come across them in your reading, if you study this subject.

When we come to the smaller divisions, then the fun really starts! Taxonomists can be divided into the 'splitters' and the 'lumpers'. The former attempt to make more genera by splitting up existing ones, because of small morphological differences between species, whilst the latter try to simplify matters by re-uniting some of the genera. This can be most confusing as nurserymen's catalogues are often out of date, and it is possible to purchase the same plant by two or more different names. Since nurserymen are not usually taxonomists, they can hardly be blamed for this.

The main reason for much of the difficulty in deciding to which genus a cactus belongs, or whether it is a new species, is because of insufficient field work. Many of the original species were described from one specimen sent to Europe. This plant may have been one from a large colony which could have varied considerably within itself. If the plant sent to Europe was from one end of this plant 'spectrum' and the next one from the opposite end, the taxonomist would probably have created a second species. Then there are always the plants in between the two extremes, so that one variable species of cactus has given rise to two or three 'new species'. The botanical explorers, such as F. Ritter, have done much to sort this out. It must be remembered, of course, that Nature does not divide plants neatly into species and genera, but has produced populations adapted to particular environments, some similar to each other and others quite different. It is man's desire to classify that has caused the difficulty, with one botanist choosing some particular characters to separate species, whilst another botanist may choose different ones.

A cultivated cactus often differs greatly in appearance from the same species growing in the desert. Some cacti have been described from cultivated material; these plants are genetically identical to those in the wild which may look completely different.

A great deal of work is being done on the classification of cacti at the present moment, both by botanists on the American continent, who are able to examine large numbers of plants in their native habitat, and by European botanists working on cultivated populations and specialised aspects, like seeds, pollen, and chromosome numbers. A great deal can be told about the relationship between plants by examining their cell structure under the microscope.

At the present moment, the classification of cacti is 'fluid', to say the least. It is likely to remain so for some time. We have tried to give the plants we are talking about their latest names, but some of them may have changed by the time this appears in print. Some are still being argued over and we could have backed the wrong name. However, a name is to most of us only something written on a label and the former '*Malacocarpus*' are no less attractive for being translated into '*Wigginsia*'. The main thing is to enjoy growing your plants; you are not collecting labels!

TWO

General Cultivation

Cacti are designed to withstand adversity and will stay alive even in old, worn-out soil. But that is no reason for ill-treating them; we do not want our plants just to stay alive, they should grow and flower. To be healthy, cacti need nourishing, well-drained soil; do not just dig old soil from the garden, but buy one of the sterilised composts that are on the market. There are some collectors who have a different compost for almost every cactus.

In the United States, the cactus enthusiast can purchase a well-mixed, nutritious soil mixture from most local nurseries. Soils not expressly designed for cacti should have some sand added, depending on the type of plant being grown. For those who mix their own, two parts of loam, two parts of coarse sand, and one part of leafmould is recommended. In any case, the soil should be loose and well-drained. Adding gravel in judicious amounts can often help.

There are many different types of pots and containers on the market. The terra cotta variety is generally available in many different sizes at reasonable cost. It drains well, so well that you must take care not to let the plants dry out. Plastic pots have their virtues, too, being lightweight (but they can tip over), colourful, and cheap, retaining water better than the clay type.

It is a good idea to repot plants annually. At the end of the year most of the mineral salts have been absorbed by the plant or leached out. Also, a young specimen needs room to stretch its roots. Before putting a plant into a new pot, scrub the pot thoroughly to eliminate any lingering bacteria or insects.

General Cultivation

Some of the older books on cacti suggest filling a third of the pot with broken crocks in order to ensure good drainage. This is nonsense; all the crocks are doing is taking up space which could be better occupied with compost, your drainage is in your compost and no amount of crocking is going to compensate for soggy soil. All that is necessary is to cover the drainage hole to prevent the soil from falling out. A good modern substitute is broken ceiling tiles, or pieces of expanded polystyrene packing, so commonly used now. This is particularly useful for plastic pots since these usually do not have a large, central drainage hole as do clay pots, but a series of smaller holes around the edge of the bottom. Just enough crushed tile or similar material can be added to cover the holes. Alternatively, fibrous peat can be used.

When the time comes to repot a cactus, it may be removed from the old pot by turning it upside down and gently tapping the edge. In the case of a clay pot with a central hole, a pencil can be pushed into it to ease out an obstinate plant; in general plants can be removed more easily from plastic pots. Several thicknesses of newspaper can be used to hold the plant if it is too spiny for the hands, but we prefer not to do this as the spines may be damaged. We find a pair of laboratory crucible tongs most useful for supporting cacti with the minimum damage to the spines. Carefully remove the old caked soil from around the base of the plant and shake any loose soil from the roots. We do not believe in pulling the roots around, but repot with the minimum disturbance. If the cactus was pot-bound it will be obvious by the masses of roots around the ball of soil, and it should be repotted in the next size of pot. If too large a pot is chosen there is a risk of damage due to the large amount of damp soil around the roots.

Worse than over-potting is under-potting. This sin is committed mainly by those who show plants. There is a limit to the pot size in many classes, so that a large plant is sometimes crammed into a 10-cm. (4-in.) pot. This does not fool the judges who know the sort of root system a healthy plant should have, and it starves the plant.

Many people think that cacti should only be repotted in the spring, but at this time of the year we are too busy seed sowing (both cacti and garden plants) to repot our collections. We do it in the latter half of the summer when the plants have finished flowering and the garden needs less attention. We can then move everything outside and deal with our plants in a leisurely manner. If you remove your plants from their old pots carefully without damaging the roots, you can repot at any time. On one or two occasions our repotting was carried on well into the winter without any harm coming to the plants. Of course spring repotting is perfectly satisfactory for those who have the time.

FERTILISERS

Some growers disapprove strongly of collectors who feed their plants. Their point of view is that fertilisers make plants large and lush, and will undoubtedly cause rot during the winter. We do not like the idea of starving plants, so we feed them. We have large plants with plenty of flowers, and our mortality rate is not high. The important thing is to choose the right fertiliser.

Plants growing in a small pot soon exhaust the nutrient in their soil, so when a plant is repotted it gets a generous pinch of bone-meal in its compost. This is slow-acting and gives the plant a continuous supply of nutrient. During the flowering season we feed the plants with a liquid fertiliser, using one suitable for tomatoes, as this has a high potassium, low nitrogen content. Fertilisers high in nitrogen cause far too much soft growth, ideal for lettuces, but not for cacti. Plants such as echinopsis and epiphyllums which produce large quantities of flowers must have a great deal taken out of them. It is up to their owners to put it back again. We feed our plants at the same time as the tomatoes, using the same strength solution. This means feeding once a fortnight between the end of June and the beginning of September. Feeding is particularly important for plants grown in soil-less composts.

It should be remembered that a lot of cacti come from lands where there is a high mineral content in the soil; many arid regions are potentially very fertile. So that even those plants which do not flower freely will be all the better for feeding, particularly if they are growing in a very sandy compost.

General Cultivation

Many of us have heard the story of the old lady who used to get her friends in Mexico to cable her every time it rained so that she would know when to water her cacti! This is an extreme case, but some people forget that their plants are living under highly artificial conditions with a restricted root run, and need a great deal more water than if their roots had the spread they have in nature.

It is impossible to lay down hard and fast rules about watering, so much depends on where the plant is situated. We would suggest that when the plant shows signs of growth, usually about March, then start watering. After that, water when the soil is dry. In fact, treat like any other pot-plant. Watering can be reduced around the end of September when the light is becoming poor. In our opinion, many cacti suffer from too little water during the summer, as their owners, thinking of the desert, are afraid to water them freely. During a really hot spell, some of our cacti receive two waterings a day, particularly those in smaller pots. In a dull, damp period, however, the plants may only receive one or two drinks a week. As mentioned elsewhere, plants in plastic pots need less frequent watering than those in the traditional clay ones.

Watering in the winter is a more difficult problem and depends on the temperature of the environment of the plants. Hardy cacti which we winter with almost no heat are kept without water from October until March. The plants in the greenhouse which are kept at a minimum of 5 °C (41 °F) are watered on sunny days, every two or three weeks, early in the morning so that any surplus water around the neck of the plant has time to dry up before evening. We find that if plants are allowed to become dust dry the root hairs may die and then there is a danger of rotting when watering starts in the spring. In any case, the plant will receive a severe check, as it is the root-hairs which absorb water and mineral salts. If it is known that a particular plant has become dust-dry in winter, with the likelihood that the root hairs have died, the first watering in spring should be given with extra caution until fresh hairs have been able to form. We have exceptions to even slight winter watering, namely the extreme desert

33

cacti, such as ariocarpus. Even our nerves fail at the prospect of watering an ariocarpus in December.

Epiphytes should certainly not be allowed to dry out completely, but should be kept slightly moist, even in the winter. Many of our epiphyllums grow late into the autumn and are showing bud in March. They have not the definite resting period of the rest of the *Cactaceae*.

Plants kept in the house are a more difficult proposition. A heated living-room has a very dry atmosphere. If left too long without water, the plant will shrivel excessively; if overwatered, it will attempt to grow when there is insufficient light for normal growth. Somehow you must balance your plants' water supply so that they remain turgid but do not form any etiolated growth. As a rough estimate we would suggest watering once a week, but this is only an average guide, individual circumstances may vary it a great deal. Again epiphytes should be kept moist and they will undoubtedly benefit and flourish in the warm atmosphere. Other cacti do best in an unheated room in winter, when very little water is needed.

The question of tap versus rain water sometimes arises. In our opinion, and also that of many growers, tap water is perfectly satisfactory. In fact, rain water, unless collected from a clean surface, and kept clean, may harbour harmful bacteria and microscopic fungi. If your tap water is exceptionally hard, it may be rather too alkaline for some cacti, especially epiphytes. This can be corrected by adding a few drops of nitric acid to each gallon of water. For the scientifically-minded, the ideal pH of the water should be rather less than the neutral 7, around pH 5–6, but in practice we find this of less importance than some growers would suggest.

We have even heard of a grower who only used boiled water for his plants. This was satisfactory when he had only a few, but as his collection expanded, he ran into practical difficulties.

TEMPERATURE

With a few exceptions cacti are not tropical plants and will survive on a minimum winter temperature of 5 °C (41 °F). To raise the temperature of your greenhouse from 5 to 10 °C (41–50 °F) will double your fuel bill. Think carefully before buying the West Indian melocactus which needs a temperature of around 15 °C (60 °F). Some of the Mexican opuntias develop brown spots on their pads if allowed to get cold, so if you find your opuntias are becoming disfigured with odd blemishes, move them as near the heater as possible.

The epiphytic cacti from the tropical rain forests would enjoy the sort of conditions that are given to orchids. However, the authors have kept many of these plants at a winter minimum of 5 °C (41 °F) without loss, but realise that they would probably flower more freely if kept warmer.

The bulk of the desert cacti need a cold, dry winter rest if they are to flower well during the summer. Our echinopsis bloom much more freely now that they have to rough it in the cold frame than they ever did in the heated greenhouse. Some cacti which will stand temperatures below freezing in the wild need a little warmth in a damp climate, otherwise they may rot.

Cacti which we have found hardy are *Notocactus, Echinopsis, Rebutia, Oreocereus, Echinocereus,* and *Chamaecereus silvestrii.* But it must be emphasised that hardiness in cacti depends to some extent on their cultivation and the situation of the greenhouse or frame. Plants which survive without heat in one greenhouse sometimes succumb to the cold in another a few streets away. If you want to try growing cacti without heat start with plants such as echinopsis or *Chamaecereus silvestrii* which form off-sets freely, so that if your experiment does not quite come off you will have a replacement for any that may die.

SITUATION

Having taken an interest in cacti and started a small collection, the first question is where are you going to keep it? Probably most of us start keeping our few plants in the living-room, and a greenhouse is not contemplated until the domestic situation becomes too difficult. Desert cacti do not make good house-plants. They come from regions of intense sun and if grown in poor light they become etiolated caricatures of their normal selves. Most of us have seen plants in shop windows which are so distorted that it is impossible to recognise the species. This does not mean that you cannot grow cacti without a greenhouse; at least one of us started with a window-sill collection.

If cacti are to be grown without a greenhouse, they must be given as much light as possible during the summer. Ideally they should be placed out of doors. If a garden or flat roof is available, the plants can be stood in the sunniest part as soon as all danger from frost is over. Otherwise an outside window ledge will do. Once the autumn rains and frosts start, the cacti must be brought inside; they need a cold winter rest, and if possible should be wintered in a cool but frost-proof room. Remember that a frost pocket can form between the curtains and the window. When you pull the curtains, make sure that your plants are on the room side. If for any reason you must keep your cacti in a room all the year round you must still give them all the light you can, remembering that the light from a window is very one-sided, and the plants need to be turned occasionally to prevent them from growing unevenly.

The easiest way to grow cacti is in a cold frame or greenhouse. For those with limited funds or space, a cold frame can be very useful. A small car heater can be used in the coldest weather, but several cacti will survive without heat, if well covered in a frame. We would suggest that if buying a cold frame, you get a mainly all-glass structure with a top that opens up completely. The plants will benefit enormously from the fresh air and sun. When siting your greenhouse or cold frame keep away from overhanging trees or shrubs which will cast shadows on it.

What we have written above applies to the usual, desert cacti, but to grow epiphytes to perfection, they really need a house to themselves, as they come from damper, more shady regions than the others. An epiphyllum house can be placed where trees give some shade from the midday sun; alternatively it can be shaded with blinds or 'Summer Cloud' coating. If, however, like most of us, you keep a mixed collection, then during the summer months, the epiphytes should be moved outdoors. They can be stood under trees where they receive broken sunlight, or placed where they will have full sun in the morning or evening, but not during the hottest part of the day.

Epiphyllums are more successful than desert cacti as houseplants. The warmer, shadier conditions agree with them, but they may need the occasional spray with water as rooms are not as moist as greenhouses. An east-facing window-sill is ideal; this gives them the early morning sun with cool, shady conditions during the rest of the day. We have a number of friends, without greenhouses, who flower epiphyllums regularly as house-plants.

BOWL GARDENS

A section on cultivation is not really complete without reference to bowl gardens. Remember that such a garden is not an ornament but a collection of living plants. All that we have said about the cultivation of pot plants applies to bowl gardens, particularly with regard to room cultivation, since of course bowl gardens are kept in rooms.

The choice of plants for a bowl garden is most important. They must all have more or less the same growing period and need the same cultural conditions. Very fast growing plants should be avoided, as they will rapidly take over the entire container. *Opuntia microdasys* var. *minima* is an ideal plant for a bowl, but the large-padded, fast-growing species would soon outgrow their welcome.

Cacti that we think look very well in bowl gardens are the small globular types, such as *Rebutia, Parodia, Notocactus* and *Mammillaria*. To give a variety of form, the less vigorous *Opuntia*, such as the varieties of *O. microdasys*, can be included.

It is not necessary for the container to have a drainage hole, provided that a good layer of gravel is placed at the bottom, and the compost is allowed to dry out between waterings, as in this case the slightest risk of over-watering must be avoided. There are plenty of attractively designed containers on the market in both pottery and various forms of plastic. Avoid the very shallow types, as they dry out too quickly and do not contain enough soil to keep the plants healthy. Some pieces of rock can be added, but go easy on the ornaments. A gaily flowering collection of rebutias does not need any competition from plastic toadstools!

Bowl gardens should be repotted annually; the compost will be exhausted after a year and over-large plants can be removed. Likewise any cacti that do not seem to be flourishing can be replaced by other species which may be more accommodating.

37

General Cultivation

Most of the 'how-to' material in this book is concerned with growing cacti under cover of some kind. There are many areas, of course, where use of these wonderful plants in the outdoor landscape is not only practical, but is eminently desirable. The Great Southwest of the United States offers the opportunity to grow hundreds of different varieties of cacti in the backyard. Even in sections where winter temperatures hover around zero for weeks at a time, cacti can be added to the outdoor environment by planting them in tubs and other containers that can be removed to warm shelter when the north winds start to blow.

Cacti for outdoor planting come in all shapes and sizes. There is the *Carnegiea gigantea* (Saguaro), which eventually grows to upwards of 30 feet (after a century or more) and the low-growing *Opuntia basilaris* (Beavertail). The opulent flowers of the *Ferocactus wislizenii* (Fishhook Barrel Cacti) are in sharp contrast to the low-key, trailing plants of the *Rhipsalis* family. In making a selection, do a rough layout of what you think you want and where, and then discuss it with your local nurseryman and with collectors in the area. Experience is the best teacher, and they will know what will grow best in your area's weather conditions.

If drainage is important to potted plants, it is probably even more important to those outdoors. A gentle slope is ideal for most cacti because it provides good runoff. On level ground you may have to mix in several parts of sand to make for a light, gritty soil. Sun is another essential. In general, cacti should be planted out of the shade.

Cacti outdoors are not difficult to care for. Water with discretion. In the summer, the plants will take more than you think they will. It is hot, the rains have come and gone, and the cacti need relief. As fall comes on, however, you must reduce the water supply to prepare the plants for their winter of rest. Dampness and cold make a combination that is deadly to many cacti. And, as has been mentioned elsewhere in connection with indoor plants, water most sparingly in the winter. Your plants are in a dormant state. Do not drown them in kindness.

General Cultivation

Fortunately, cacti do not suffer greatly from these troubles. There are two pests, however, related to the cochineal insect, which are without doubt the most troublesome. These are the mealy bug and root mealy bug, both belonging to the genus *Rhizococcus*. Mealy bugs are tiny creatures, about 2–3 mm. ($\frac{1}{16}$–$\frac{1}{8}$ in.) long, looking rather like miniature, white wood lice. The eggs are laid within small, cotton-wool-like cocoons which are sometimes seen on the stems of plants and may not be associated by beginners with the adult creatures; experienced growers will be only too familiar with both. The pests feed by sucking the sap of the plants, and if left unattended, can multiply with such rapidity that they can cause serious disfiguration, particularly of young growth. When the collection consists of only a few plants on a window-sill, which can be examined frequently, the odd mealy bug is easily dealt with by pricking off with tweezers or squashing with a match stick (their bodies are very soft). A larger greenhouse collection, however, is a different matter, and at the first sign of the pest it will probably be necessary to spray. One of the most effective sprays is nicotine sulphate. Great care must be taken when using and storing this poison. Some growers use a malathion preparation for the control of mealy bug. Personally, we are not very keen on this as we maintain mixed collections of cacti and other succulents and malathion can damage some of the latter, particularly crassulas. It is, however, very effective. Various proprietary preparations of malathion can be obtained from horticultural sundriesmen. From the same source may also be obtained preparations containing the pesticide dimethoate. This acts partly as a systemic pesticide, and partly by contact. It can, therefore, be both sprayed on to the plants and watered into the soil. Systemic materials act by entering the sap via the roots and rendering it fatal to sucking pests.

Root mealy bugs are more troublesome since they are seldom seen, except by repotting, and the first sign above ground is a sickly plant. They are rather smaller than the ordinary variety, and as the name implies, are confined to the roots of the plants, where their presence is indicated by ashy deposits. When these are noticed, all the infected soil must be removed and the roots

39

treated with one of the pesticides mentioned above. An occasional watering with a nicotine or a dimethoate preparation will help to keep this pest at bay.

If the collection is not too large, annual repotting is the best way of bringing the activities of root mealy bug to light. When repotting, a few crystals of paradichlorobenzene added to the crocks at the bottom of the pot will help to discourage these and other pests. This is a standard household material as a moth deterrent, and can be obtained quite easily and cheaply.

Although mealy bugs are by far the most common pests of cacti, there are others which must be mentioned.

Scale insects are related to mealy bugs but form a small scab with a dark centre. This is the pest itself, which can be seen if the scale is removed. If the attack is small and local the scabs can be picked off, otherwise one of the preparations already mentioned can be used.

Red spider mite is sometimes a pest in collections, particularly when the atmosphere is very dry. It is not a true spider, but a minute mite, reddish in colour. Its fine webs can be seen between the spines. A nicotine or malathion spray will control it, but it can be troublesome if allowed to get a hold.

A pest that is particularly damaging to seedlings is the sciarid fly, of which there are several species with various common names, such as fungus gnats, mushroom flies, or tomato flies. The adults are minute dark or black flies, sometimes seen hovering over seedpans. The flies themselves are harmless, but the larvae feed on vegetable matter, both rotting and living. Seedlings are often eaten at soil level, and topple over, leaving a hollow shell. A gamma-BHC dust is effective against the flies, but the larvae and eggs are best treated with a dimethoate or malathion preparation, or nicotine.

The above are the most frequently met pests of cacti; occasionally snails and slugs may cause trouble in collections. All gardeners are familiar with these pests, and there are many preparations on the market to deal with them. Greenhouse hygiene is the best preventative for all pests. An annual clean-out, preferably in spring, when the staging and floor should be scrubbed down with a disinfectant, will help to discourage unwanted lodgers.

General Cultivation

The only disease that the cactus collector is likely to meet is rot, caused by fungal or bacterial infection. This is usually seen as a brownish or blackish discoloration on the stems, and must be cut out immediately. When doing this, it is important to cut right back to healthy tissue, carefully removing any brown or orange spots as these indicate remaining infection and, if left, will spread again. As a further precaution, the cut surface can be dusted with flowers of sulphur.

If a plant rots at the base, it is usually a sign of poor drainage around the base of the plant, sometimes due in turn to caked compost. Pest damage at soil level will also often initiate rot. The only remedy when this happens is to cut off the healthy part of the plant and treat as described under 'cuttings'. Rot occasionally affects the roots of a cactus, particularly in the case of the 'rare' imported plants, which can suddenly lose their roots without apparent reason. Again, all infected tissue must be removed, and the top either treated as a cutting or grafted.

Mention must be made here of some conditions which are sometimes mistaken for infections or pests. Brown corky patches appearing on the stems of some cacti, notably the larger, trunk-forming ones, are quite normal. Corky spots or patches on other plants have several causes. Poor ventilation in summer, too sudden falls in temperature in winter, or mechanical damage can all be responsible. Deficiency of certain materials in the compost, such as nitrogen or phosphorus, may also cause marking of the stems, as will excess nitrogen with some plants, particularly certain epiphyllums. The remedy for this is a good, balanced compost, together possibly with suitable feeding from time to time. The marked stems are usually permanently disfigured; cuttings are then needed to produce once more an attractive specimen.

THREE

Propagation

Sooner or later the cactus collector will no doubt wish to try his hand at raising from seed. This is much cheaper than buying new plants, although of course it takes longer. But there are two definite advantages in raising cacti from seed; firstly the plants supplied by the average nurseryman are very limited in variety, seed specialists offering a much wider choice, and secondly, if you grow a plant from seed it is far more likely to produce an unmarked specimen than one brought from a nursery. There is of course a snag. Cactus seed germination is very variable and unless it is fairly fresh, the results may be zero. However, every hobby has its setbacks and the thrill of having produced your own plants from a minute seed greatly outweighs any of the frustrations.

Probably no aspect of cactus growing shows such a personal variation of methods as seed raising. We have tried most of them, having sown seed in commercial seed compost, vermiculite, peat, leafmould and sand, and even broken brick. Each of these methods has its advocates, but in our opinion, provided a few basic requirements are met, the actual seed compost used is of little importance. We shall describe the method we prefer to use at the moment, but we certainly do not claim that this is the best; it just happens to suit us. In your reading and discussions with other enthusiasts you will come across different methods; by all means consider them and use them if you prefer, but too frequent changing from one method to another, without a fair trial, is not likely to give best results.

The first requirement is good, fresh seed. This is largely outside your control, unless you produce seed from your own

Propagation

plants, which does not help in the acquisition of new specimens to add to the collection. In many cases we have had zero germination from bought seed, whilst getting 100 per cent from our own, fresh seed. Do not always blame the supplier; he is very much at the mercy of the professional seed collector in receiving fresh seed promptly. We suspect, however, that some seed merchants keep seed longer than they should in the hope of selling it next year. If you only want to try your hand at raising cacti from seed, without bothering about particular types, you may prefer to start with a packet of mixed seed usually offered by the large, 'general', well-known seed merchants. Later you will probably wish to deal with one of the specialists in cactus seeds.

The next requirements are warmth and moisture. Cactus seed needs a temperature of 21–27 °C (70–80 °F) for successful germination; although it will sometimes germinate at a lower temperature, it takes much longer and may well rot before it does so. Often a suitable temperature can be produced in an airing cupboard, but although light is not needed for germination, once the seedlings appear they must be gradually exposed to light, without too much drop in temperature, and in the early part of the year this may prove difficult or impossible. The owners of a heated seed propagator will, of course, have no trouble in this respect. With a propagator controlled at 24 °C (75 °F) we like to sow our seed early in the spring, usually during late February or March. This depends to some extent on the arrival of the seedsmen's lists, and often seed has to be sown later. If you have no propagator, it is better to wait until the weather warms up, depending on your location. An advantage of early sowing is that the seedlings do not run the risk of exposure to the summer sun in their very early stages.

A cactus seed compost should retain its moisture without becoming soggy. Also, it should be reasonably sterile. We mentioned earlier the various seed composts that have been suggested by different growers; probably the simplest is 40 per cent soil, 40 per cent coarse sand and 20 per cent leafmould. This is quite satisfactory, but we have also found that it tends to cake somewhat, and now use a proprietary brand of peat seed compost. This peat contains added nutrients which are sufficient to last until the seedlings need to be transplanted. We have

43

had the best results so far with this material. We use mostly plastic sandwich boxes for seed raising, a number of small holes having first been bored in the bottom. There is no need for further drainage with the peat compost, which is put into the container to within about 1 cm. ($\frac{3}{8}$ in.) from the top, levelled and gently tapped down. Since about twenty different types of seed can be sown in one container, divisions are made by pressing plastic plant labels horizontally into the compost to form about four rows. Separations within the rows are made with T labels on which the names of the seeds are written with horticultural ink. The seed pan is then stood in water until the compost is thoroughly wet. A few crystals of potassium permanganate dissolved in the water to give just a pink colour will help to disinfect the compost.

After allowing the pan to drain for a few minutes, a thin layer of peat is sifted over the surface, using a kitchen flour sieve. This gives a fine, porous surface to receive the seeds, and is not afterwards touched or pressed in any way. This is the reason for putting the labels in first; if pressed in at this stage depressions will be made in the compost in which small seeds will be lost. The seeds are then sprinkled into each prepared compartment, distributing them as evenly as possible. The best way to do this is to use a folded strip of paper into which the seeds are first tipped; by holding the strip in one hand and gently tapping with the forefinger of the other, even distribution is made easier. The seeds are not covered with any further peat. Most cactus seed is small, some, such as parodia, extremely minute and dust-like; this is the reason for the finely sifted surface since, if the compost is coarse, tiny seeds can easily slip into a 'crevasse' and be completely smothered. Some cactus seeds, such as opuntia, are quite large and these can be placed individually with tweezers, pressing them into the surface.

This peat compost retains moisture well, but if it does dry out, it is difficult to moisten again. However, seed compost should never be allowed to dry out completely. When sown, the plastic box lid is put on to conserve moisture. If another type of container has been used, such as a small plastic pot for just a few seeds, it is either covered with a piece of glass or put into a plastic bag, the top of which is closed with a rubber band. We then put the container in a propagator which is well shaded from direct sunlight. Although some growers keep the pans or pots sealed in a plastic bag until the seedlings are quite large, we prefer to give a little ventilation by slightly raising the lid when a fair proportion of the seed has germinated. We keep the young plants shaded during the whole of their first year since too much strong light will cause them to become reddish in colour, and when this happens, they usually stop growing. Further watering can be done by soaking as before, but whilst the pan is kept covered it will rarely be necessary. The box must be kept well-drained.

The time taken for cactus seed to germinate is very variable, depending on the temperature, the freshness of the seed, and its type. It may vary from a few days to a month or more, but under our conditions we hope to see the seedlings within a fortnight. Some writers claim to have had a germination a year after sowing. We do not, of course, deny the truth of this, but it has never been our experience. After about a month we lose hope. In practice, what generally happens is that a few of several varieties sown will germinate fairly quickly and the rest will appear over a longer period of time. If more ventilation is to be given on germination, as we like to do, we have to consider either those that are up, or those yet to come. We ventilate after 10–14 days, when most of the ones we can hope for are showing. Some cactus seedlings, such as opuntia, look very much like those of many ordinary garden plants, having definite cotyledons, between which the tiny, bristly spines later appear, whilst most others are little green balls to start with; they elongate later.

The growth of moss in seedpans is sometimes troublesome. Moss around plants out of the seedling stage is a sign either of overwatering, or poor drainage, or both, but since seedlings must be kept moist, it is often difficult to avoid. It does not actually harm cacti, but can easily smother the smaller seedlings. Moss may be kept in check by sprinkling a little silver sand over the surface as soon as it appears. This should be just sufficient to cover the moss but not the cacti; as the latter grow the depth of the sand can be increased. Pests and diseases of seedlings are dealt with in the section on that subject.

Unless growth is very rapid the seedlings can remain in the same container for about a year, when they can be pricked out the

Propagation

following spring into the 'adult' compost. Care should be taken not to damage the fine roots when doing so. In any case, the seedlings should not be moved until they are of a manageable size; just what this size is will depend on the size of your fingers and your manual dexterity. Sometimes a pair of blunt-ended tweezers will help.

It is quite possible to obtain seed from one's own plants. Some cacti are self-fertile and will usually set seed readily, it is merely a matter of deciding when it is ripe. The pods of most cacti will be ready for removal in the autumn, when some, such as rebutia, will often burst open, scattering the seed in the pot around the parent plant. Mammillarias, however, retain their seed-pods for a long time, often not being ripe until the following year. If, on examination, the seeds are found to be black, it is likely that they are ready for harvesting.

Self-sterile cacti will only set seed if pollinated by another plant with flowers open at the same time. If several species of the particular genus are flowering together, possible pollination can be left to insects and chance, if you are not concerned about the parentage of the eventual seedlings. Otherwise, the plants to be crossed can be segregated and pollination effected by means of a small brush.

With regard to which cacti are self-fertile and which self-sterile, it is difficult to make a hard and fast division, for different growers have differing ideas on the subject, depending upon their personal experiences, and, possibly, particular conditions. In our experience, self-fertile plants include *Notocactus*, some *Rebutia* (but not all), *Lobivia oyonica*, many *Mammillaria*, *Lophophora*, *Wigginsia* and *Pfeiffera*. The plants we have found to be generally self-sterile are *Echinopsis*, usually *Parodia*, *Astrophytum*, *Epiphyllum* and *Schlumbergera*.

Some cactus seed-pods, such as rebutia, when opened, display masses of dry seed, whilst others, notably pfeiffera and epiphyllum, contain a sticky pulp in which the seeds are embedded. This can be washed under a tap in a kitchen strainer to dispose of most of the pulp. The seeds are then removed and spread on blotting paper to dry. When quite dry they can be stored in envelopes until ready to sow. Generally speaking, home-produced seed germinates very well.

46

Propagation

Although raising cacti from seed is the ideal way to add to the variety of the collection, even if slowly, propagation by means of cuttings is the simplest method of increasing the number of plants. This is often useful for producing extra plants for exchange with other collectors, or even for sale if one has the space to propagate in quantity. Also, the occasional sick plant can often be saved by removing the remaining healthy parts and treating them as cuttings.

From the point of view of producing suitable growth for cuttings, cacti may be divided into several classes. Firstly, there are the plants forming off-sets readily. These are miniature versions of the adult produced from the main plant, and sometimes appear already equipped with roots. They are, strictly speaking, not cuttings at all and only need to be pulled away from the parent plant and potted up. Some *Echinopsis* and *Lobivia* produce off-sets in this way. Other *Echinopsis, Rebutia, Parodia* and *Mammillaria* form off-sets which have no roots and need to be cut away from the parent with a small sharp knife. Some *Parodia* and *Gymnocalycium*, together with *Notocactus, Astrophytum* and *Wigginsia*, have never produced off-sets with us.

Branching cacti, such as opuntias and epiphyllums, can be propagated by removing at a convenient joint. An opuntia joint or 'pad' can be easily cut away; in the case of a more woody epiphyllum it is often necessary to resort to secateurs.

Finally, we have those cacti, notably the columnar *Cereus*, including *Trichocereus*, which normally do not produce any branches, at least not in their younger, smaller stages. Naturally one would not wish to mutilate a fine specimen cereus by cutting it, but sometimes it is necessary or desirable to do so. The most usual reason in the case of one of these plants is simply that it is growing too tall for the greenhouse. In this case a portion of suitable length can be cut off and re-rooted. The remaining part will usually then send out branches from around the cut surface. When a few inches long, these can be removed and treated as cuttings. This may often be put to advantage in the case of *Opuntia cylindrica*, which normally forms a tall, straight column. If cut 15–30 cm. (6–12 in.) from the base, a smaller branched plant will eventually result; the top can be re-rooted. Should a cereus or similar plant have become damaged and disfigured on the lower part of the stem, the intact upper portion can be removed, rooted, and a fresh start made.

The main difference between cuttings of cacti and those of most other plants is that cactus cuttings must be left unpotted to allow the cut surface to form a callus, otherwise rotting will probably occur. This 'drying-out time' will vary from one or two days for a small cut surface, such as an opuntia pad or a narrow-necked off-set, to five days or a week for larger sections, the longest time being needed for a large-stemmed cereus. Some growers suggest dusting the cut surface with flowers of sulphur to prevent fungus attack, but we have not found this to be necessary. When the surface has dried and callused over, the cutting is potted up in a very sandy compost which should be kept just moist. Commencement of growth usually indicates that rooting has taken place; some plants root much more quickly than others. The best time to take any cuttings is during the maximum growth (generally May and June), although it can be done at other times if necessary. Should a cutting be taken in winter in order to save a part of a sick plant, it is best to keep the cut portion until spring before potting up and attempting to root it.

The primitive cacti, *Pereskia*, are the only exceptions to the 'drying-off' period for cuttings. These cacti are treated in the same manner as other plants, the cuttings being potted up at once.

GRAFTING

There are those growers and hobbyists who think that grafting is the most desirable method of propagation. There are others who think that it is as unnatural as a plastic bowl garden. On two points there is general agreement: grafting is not uncomplicated, and grafting can produce some most interesting and unusual shapes. The authors of this book do graft, and for three reasons. Firstly, there are those cacti which never really seem to thrive on their own roots with us in this country, probably because they are particularly exacting in their demands with regard to soil and conditions. These are all better grown grafted.

Comparison of a cactus and 'other' succulent. A cactus (cereus) on left, and a euphorbia on right. An example of parallel evolution; the two plants are similar in form, but only the cactus has areoles

Mealy bugs. The commonest pest of cacti in cultivation

Mealy bug eggs under 'wool'

Close-up of mealy bug

A bowl garden

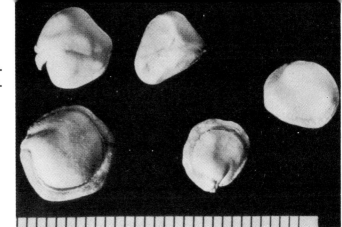

Opuntia seeds.
Scale in mm.

DEVELOPMENT OF
OPUNTIA SEEDLINGS
(*left*) Only cotyledons
showing
(*centre*) The first spines
appear
(*right*) A small joint or
pad

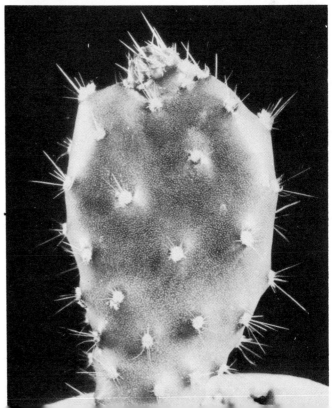

Young opuntia

GRAFTING
(*top left*) Preparing the stock
(*top right*) Shaping the stock
(*centre left*) Shaping the scion
(*above*) The scion in position
(*left*) Removing part of the scion to
produce off-sets on remainder

Cutting a slot in the
opuntia

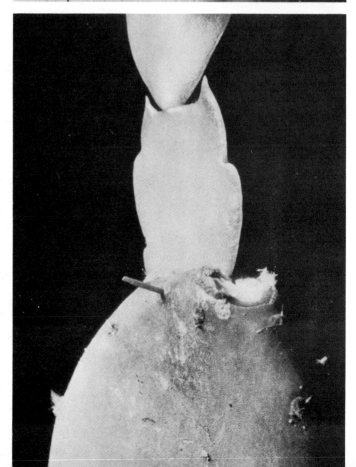

The scion pinned in,
using a spine as pin

Pereskia aculeata.
Young specimen grown
from a cutting

Pereskiopsis spathulata

Quiabentia zehntneri

Opuntia subulata. Top of a large plant, showing pointed, cylindrical leaves

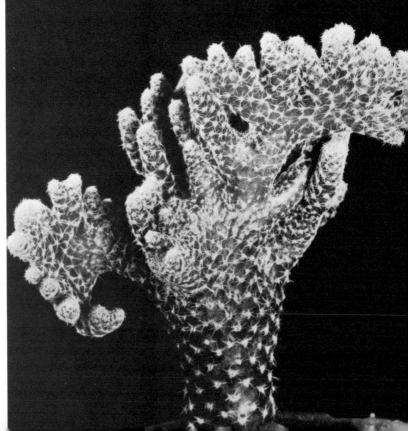

Opuntia spegazzinii, flowering in a 7.5 cm. (3 in.) pot

Opuntia diademata

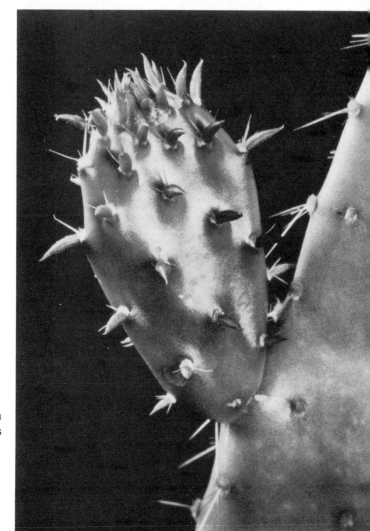

Opuntia clavarioides

Young opuntia pad with small leaves

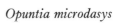

Opuntia microdasys

Opuntia microdasys var. *rufida*

Opuntia paraguayensis

Carnegiea gigantea in habitat. A mature plant growing in California

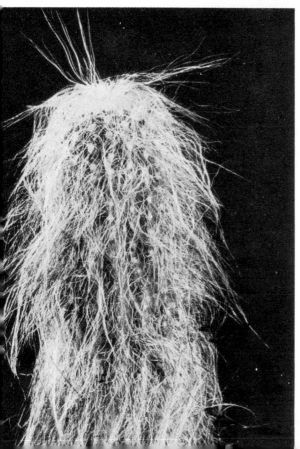

Cephalocereus senilis. A young pot plant

Pilosocereus palmeri. A large specimen in cultivation

Stetsonia coryne

(*above*) *Echinocactus grusonii*. A flowering specimen in the Argotti
Gardens, Malta
(*below*) *Ferocactus acanthodes*

Cleistocactus strausii

Denmoza erythrocephala

Machaerocereus eruca.
The upturned end of a
plant in cultivation

Melocactus communis

Oreocereus celsianus. A young specimen

Propagation

Secondly, a plant may never have developed a good root system, possibly due to incorrect treatment at some time. Some young cacti bought from nurserymen have either poor roots or a narrow constricting 'neck'. With these we cut off the roots and neck, and graft, keeping the plant on the graft until it has fully recovered, when it can be removed and rooted as for a cutting. Thirdly, we graft in order to propagate the rarer cacti which do not form off-sets readily.

When a plant has become well established on a graft and has made sufficient growth it can be cut off, leaving a substantial portion on the stock. This will eventually send out off-sets, which can later be removed and grafted in their turn. The larger, top portion may be either rooted or re-grafted. This is one of the most rapid methods of propagation, and is the reason for much of the current grafting. Many of the rarer cacti, difficult to obtain in this country, are freely multiplied by nurserymen using this method.

For the most usual case of grafting a globular or cylindrical plant, a good stock is one of the less spiny *T. richocereus*, such as *T. spachianus*. For small plants or off-sets, eriocerei are very useful. The main consideration is that the stock should be a plant that roots and grows readily itself, and we prefer it to be well rooted, although some growers graft on unrooted cuttings.

With a razor blade, we cut across the stock 2·5 or 5 cm. (1 or 2 in.) from the base; the top part can be treated as a cutting for future use. The square edge is chamfered (this reduces the risk of the surfaces becoming concave and pushing off the graft), and a further thin slice cut and left in place to prevent the surface from drying. The scion is next cut and chamfered, the slice from the stock removed, and the two cut surfaces pressed together. By a slight rubbing movement, air is excluded. The two must be held together; we do this by means of two rubber bands of a suitable length passed around the pot and over the scion. If necessary, the top of the scion may be protected by means of a small pad of cotton wool. The grafted plant should be left undisturbed for about two weeks; it should be placed in a warm, shady part of the greenhouse and the stock watered with the other cacti. After this time, the rubber bands are carefully removed, when the grafted plant can take its place with the rest

49

of the collection. It should, however, be carefully watched for a while for any sign of the graft not having taken. If so, it will come off with a gentle touch; once growth starts all should be well. If it does not take, the process must be repeated. As for cuttings, the best time for grafting is during the growing season, spring and early summer.

For flat-stemmed cacti, such as *Epiphyllum, Rhipsalidopsis* and *Schlumbergera*, the wedge graft may be used. A suitable stock in this case is an opuntia pad. A slit is cut in the edge of the pad with a sharp knife, the end of the scion cut to a narrow wedge shape, and pushed into the slit. To hold it in place we pin it with a spine from an opuntia, which does not corrode as would a pin or needle.

Schlumbergera and *Rhipsalidopsis* are sometimes grafted on to the top of a pereskia stem; this gives a 'standard' effect. These should then preferably be grown at a temperature of 10 °C (50 °F) because of the more tender stock.

The flat-stemmed cacti do not usually need grafting for the reasons mentioned at the beginning of this section, since they root readily and grow easily on their own roots, but for those who like to experiment, it may be interesting to try a few. However, for us, this is 'grafting for the sake of grafting', and as implied at the beginning, we personally are not very interested in this.

FOUR

Primitive Cacti

TRIBE PERESKIEAE

Pereskia

With their rose-like flowers, pereskias are the most primitive of the *Cactaceae*, and the least succulent cacti. They are shrubby or climbing plants with woody stems, large leaves and many spines. On close inspection, it will be found that the leaves and spines arise from areoles, those small cushion-like structures which distinguish the *Cactaceae* from all other families of plants. The flowers are white or pale pink, and are often sweetly perfumed; the petals are not joined into a tube as in most other species of cacti. This, combined with its pale colouring, gives the flower a superficial resemblance to a wild rose.

These plants are found in the moist tropical regions of America. It is very difficult to say exactly where a given species of pereskia originated, as the Indians have used them as hedging for many centuries, and the plants remain when the village huts have crumbled and the cultivated fields have returned to the wild. They were probably the first cultivated cacti.

In cultivation, pereskias are at their best if planted in a greenhouse border where there is plenty of root room. Large specimens will flower. Young ones can be grown successfully as pot plants, and replaced with cuttings when they have outgrown their accommodation. Pereskia cuttings should not be dried but potted up immediately. These cacti should be watered generously in the summer, and kept from drying out completely in winter. Under the rather cold conditions found in most cactus houses, 4–5 °C (40 °F), pereskias lose their leaves in the autumn. Ideally they should have a higher temperature up to 10 °C (50 °F). They can be grown quite easily from seed which is available from the specialist seedsmen. Plants are not often offered for sale, presumably because there is little demand for them, and they do not travel as well as their more succulent relatives. However, at least one is worth growing as a curiosity, it being difficult to convince the uninitiated that it is in fact a cactus. *Pereskia aculeata* is a large climbing shrub which is found from Florida down through Mexico to Argentina. The flowers are whitish and sweetly perfumed. The variety *rubescens* (sometimes known as *P. godseffiana*) has variegated red leaves. *P. saccharosa* is an erect shrub from Argentina and Paraguay. It will reach a height of about 4·5 m. (15 ft.) and has pink flowers. Other erect, shrub-like species are *P. bleo*, *P. conzattii*, and *P. grandifolia*.

Maihuenia

This genus is included by some authors with the *Opuntieae* and by others with the *Pereskieae*. Since these plants do not carry glochids, it seems logical to include them with the latter. The plants closely resemble *Tephrocactus* in appearance, but have persistent, cylindrical leaves. They are rare in cultivation; the species most likely to be met is *Maihuenia poeppigii*. This is a hardy plant from the hills of Chile with oval joints covered with white spines. The flowers are yellow, but these high-altitude cacti are often very difficult to flower in cultivation.

TRIBE OPUNTIEAE

Pereskiopsis

With the *Pereskiopsis* we enter the tribe of the *Opuntieae*, characterised by the presence of glochids in the areoles. These are minute barbed bristles, seen to perfection in *Opuntia microdasys*. This spineless plant looks quite harmless, but if the hand is brushed against a pad it will pick up dozens of tiny irritating hairs. If these are not removed, and being light-coloured, they are easy to overlook, small festering spots will appear on the skin. So treat the *Opuntieae* with respect.

The pereskiopsis resemble the pereskias; they, too, are branched shrubs, but rather smaller than the latter, with fleshier stems and leaves. Where they differ from the pereskias is in the presence of glochids in the areoles. Being somewhat succulent, the pereskiopsis are able to spread into the drier regions of Mexico and Baja California.

There are at least 11 species of pereskiopsis; the one occasionally offered for sale in this country is *P. spathulata*. This is a small shrub with leaves up to 5 cm. (2 in.) long. In our experience, it is not particularly easy to cultivate.

In addition to pereskiopsis there are three other, rather primitive genera which are not often seen in cultivation, but occasionally their names appear in seed lists or plant catalogues, and it is useful to know something about them.

Quiabentia

These are South American shrubs, rather straggly in habit, with fleshy, cylindrical stems and oval leaves. *Quiabentia pflanzii* is a tree which may reach a height of 12 m. (40 ft.) in nature. *Q. zehntneri* is a bush about 2 m. (6 ft.) high with small rounded leaves, 2–3 cm. (1 in.) long. There are many small slender whitish spines, and the red flowers are produced in the autumn.

Pterocactus

These plants are mainly found in Patagonia. The cylindrical, succulent stems arise from a tuberous root. In cultivation, if the plant is allowed to become dry the stems will wither and fall off. Once conditions become moister, the tuber sends up new shoots. In this genus, the leaves are rudimentary and soon shrivel. The species occasionally offered for sale is *Pterocactus kuntzei*. It is said to have yellow flowers, but we have never seen it in bloom.

Primitive Cacti

Tacinga

The two rare species in this genus are found in the scrublands around Bahia in Brazil. They are climbing shrubs whose rudimentary leaves are soon shed. The flowers are nocturnal.

Opuntia

The genus *Opuntia* can be sub-divided into three subgenera, *Cylindropuntia, Tephrocactus* and *Opuntia.*

(a) *Cylindropuntia*

It is a short step from the pereskiopsis with its thickened stem to *Opuntia subulata,* bearing fleshy leaves on top of stout, cylindrical stems. In this particular species of opuntia the leaves may reach a length of 10 cm. (4 in.) and persist for some weeks. Early botanists included it with *Pereskia* but the half-cylindrical leaves are carried only on the new growth, and of course the glochids leave no doubt that this plant is an opuntia. Other cylindrical opuntias which have definite leaves on the new growth are *O. cylindrica, O. vestita,* and *O. verschaffeltii.* As we shall see later on, some other opuntias have small leaves on new growth, but these are very soon lost.

The cylindrical opuntias are found both in North and South America; those from the Southern Hemisphere are sometimes referred to by the somewhat unwieldy name of *Austrocylindropuntia.* They vary in form from small bushy shrubs to almost tree-like plants; these latter are best left to the owners of very large greenhouses. Opuntias like ample root room and should be generously potted in a fairly rich compost. With the exception of *O. salmiana* and *O. verschaffeltii,* these plants are not easy to flower as pot plants. This variety is lovely in full bloom. In the warmer, drier climates it can be used outdoors to great effectiveness. Plantings in public gardens as far away as Barcelona are famed for their beauty.

The 'Chollas' are included in this section. Cholla is a Spanish word meaning 'head-shaped' and is applied to the cylindrical-jointed opuntias; the top of a large specimen, with its masses of branched joints, often resembles a human head. They are usually viciously spined, and although feared by man and shunned by many of the desert animals, at least two of the latter have come to terms with them to gain protection. The Cactus Wren lives and nests amongst the furiously armed branches, and a small desert rodent, the kangaroo rat, somehow manages to construct its home from masses of the cholla joints, living inside a mound of them. Few predators dare to enter. Typical chollas are *O. acanthocarpa, O. bigelowii, O. imbricata, O. tunicata.*

O. acanthocarpa is found from Utah to Mexico, and in the wild makes a plant up to 2 m. (6 ft.) in height. The young growth has noticeable leaves. The flowers are pink.

O. bigelowii is a North American opuntia, and in the wild is a formidable plant with its numerous stout, pale yellow spines. Owing to the ease with which these opuntias shed their joints, it is known as the Jumping Cholla. The joints, when fallen, make an almost impassable barrier for horses and many other animals. This cholla is the one mainly used by the kangaroo rat for its home. In spite of its vicious nature, *O. bigelowii* is one of the most attractive of the desert plants. In order to produce the beautiful spines of the wild specimens, the light must be intense and prolonged. When imported, it may well have magnificent spines on the old stems, but those grown in cultivation are usually insignificant by comparison. *O. bigelowii* is a smallish shrub with joints about 5–15 cm. (2–6 in.) long, and green-centred white flowers.

O. clavarioides, or the 'Nigger's-hand', is included amongst the cylindrical opuntias, although at first glance it does not seem to bear very much resemblance to other members of the group. This native of Chile is exceedingly slow growing on its own roots, which are large and tuberous, and is usually grafted on to one of the more robust species of opuntia, or trichocereus. Ungrafted, the joints are cylindrical, some of them ending in a fan-shaped growth. Grafting seems to increase the tendency to form cristate growths, and many convoluted joints are formed. Grafted plants do sometimes flower in cultivation; growers in this country have described the flower colour as yellowish-brown.

O. cylindrica is very frequently seen in collections; it is found in Ecuador and Peru. This species will form a column up to 2 m.

(6 ft.) in height, but if beheaded, the base will send out side branches, giving a very attractive candelabra effect. The flowers are red. There is a cristate form of this plant which is frequently seen and quite easy to grow.

O. imbricata is a native of the region Mexico to Colorado. It is one of the tree-like opuntias and will eventually form a specimen 3 m. (10 ft.) high in nature. It has beautiful yellow spines and reddish flowers, although it is quite a variable species even in the wild state.

O. leptocaulis spreads from Texas and Arizona down into Mexico. It forms a densely branched bush of slender, almost pencil-like joints.

O. pachypus is one of the most desirable of all the opuntias, and also one of the most difficult to acquire. It is found in Peru where it reaches a height of almost 1 m. (39 in.). It is a very slow-growing plant, usually unbranched, and covered with numerous white spines. The flowers are scarlet.

O. salmiana is one of the two opuntias that can be brought into bloom in a 5-cm. (2-in.) pot. This little South American has slender branches with a few yellowish spines. It will eventually reach a height of about 1 m. (39 in.), but specimens grown in small pots usually make about 30 cm. (1 ft.). The flowers are whitish-yellow and followed by red fruit. These contain no viable seeds, but sprout small joints from the areoles; they eventually fall off and root.

O. spegazzinii is a variety of the above and equally easy to flower. The stems are smoother and the spines very insignificant. The flowers are white.

O. subulata is found in Chile and Argentina. It is a strong growing plant, forming a column up to about 4·5 m. (15 ft.) high. It eventually branches and is a much sturdier plant than *O. cylin-drica*. In cultivation, it grows very rapidly and is difficult to keep within bounds. A specimen belonging to one of the authors has to be cut down from time to time to prevent it reaching the top of the greenhouse. This necessitates the use of a saw, but the procedure is quite satisfactory as the top portion can be rooted to form a short, thick column, until it once again outgrows the available height. The lower part, cut into sections, is also rooted; these form good branching plants which can be given away or exchanged. The flower colour of *O. subulata*, although seldom seen, is red.

O. tunicata is found in Mexico, Ecuador and Chile. It was originally called *O. furiosa*, which presumably sums up the discoverer's feelings about this spiny plant. It is a much-branched bush about 60 cm. (2 ft.) high, and because of its small size it makes a very good pot plant. The joints are about 15 cm. (6 in.) long, covered with spines which in the wild are 5 cm. (2 in.) long. Even in cultivation the spines are prominent and very beautiful, but the plant is to be treated with respect.

O. verschaffeltii comes from northern Bolivia and is not too difficult to flower in cultivation. The flowers are dark red. This is a slow-growing plant which makes a bush about 30 cm. (1 ft.) in height. The stems are slender and the individual joints about 15 cm. (6 in.) long. The spines are thin, almost hair-like.

O. vestita is from Bolivia and is covered with long white spines and white hair. This plant should be watched carefully since the white hair makes a perfect hiding place for mealy bug. There is a cristate form which is even more prone to harbour these pests. The plant reaches a height of about 60 cm. (2 ft.) and has dark red flowers.

(b) *Tephrocactus*

Some botanists consider that the dwarf, globular opuntias of South America are a development of the *Cylindropuntia*. Certainly, their joints can be considered as thickened cylinders. These are the alpines of the opuntia world and, like many high altitude plants, they are smaller versions of their relatives of the plains. They are excellent plants for the collector with little space to spare but who wishes to grow some opuntias. Most of them can be grown healthily in a 7·5-cm. (3-in.) half pot or pan. Many of them spread out in a cushion-like manner and do better in a shallow container. Being plants of the hills, they are much hardier than many of the larger opuntias and will survive low temperatures if kept dry. They should be grown in an open compost and put in a position where they get the maximum light. We have never heard of a tephrocactus flowering in northern climes, although many must be of sufficient size. This is presumably due to lack of sunlight, the intensity of light needed to stimulate bud formation never being reached at this latitude and altitude. This is not a great disadvantage since comparatively few growers do flower their opuntias. For some reason, tephrocacti are not as easy to come by as many of the opuntias, but there are sufficient species around to make an interesting small collection, and the position may improve. Fashions in plants change; one day all the collectors in South America may be exporting miniature opuntias.

The joints of many of these tephrocacti are very loosely attached and it is quite easy to detach one accidentally. These joints will root very readily, and in the native state, broken-off joints are probably blown around by the wind or carried on animals' fur, enabling the cactus to propagate itself vegetatively. The joints carry very tiny, awl-like leaves on the new growth; these soon shrivel and drop off.

Seeds of these opuntias are sometimes available. It is usual to sow them in the autumn and place the seed pan outside, exposing the seeds to frost and snow. In the event of there being no cold weather, some growers press the refrigerator into service. Without this cold treatment, which follows the natural conditions of the plant, germination is far less likely to take place.

O. andicola forms a low, spreading clump; the long spines are white.

O. diademata (syn. O. glomerata) has greyish-green joints, which on an imported specimen may be up to 7·5 cm. (3 in.) long. We have never been able to reproduce such a size in cultivation. The spines are long and papery. This is not a caespitose plant and as joints are very weakly attached to one another, it is quite difficult to keep a large specimen.

O. floccosa has joints up to 15 cm. (6 in.) high covered in white hair, which gives it a superficial resemblance to *Oreocereus trollii*. However, underneath the silky coat are the glochids waiting for the unwary. This is not the easiest of the tephrocacti to grow.

O. ovata forms a cushion of oval joints; these are bright green in colour and have yellowish spines.

O. pentlandii is a very pretty plant with particularly bright green joints, and very large yellow areoles. This is a cushion-forming plant, the mound may be up to 15 cm. (6 in.) high.

O. platyacantha is a spreading plant with elongated joints of a beautiful bronze-brown colour. Some of the spines are papery but less attractive than those of *O. diademata*.

O. russellii is a small bush; the joints are a dull green colour, and are very spiny, particularly on the top.

O. sphaerica, again a small bush, with almost spherical joints, yellow areoles and white spines. Some of the plants offered for sale under this name are probably *O. ovata*.

O. strobiliformis is an unusual-looking plant with joints shaped like pine cones (hence the name). Unfortunately we have never been able to grow plants with joints as large as those on the original imported plant. The erect joints are of a green-grey colour and almost spineless; one of the easiest to handle of the opuntias.

O. subinermis is a cushion-shaped plant with olive-green joints almost devoid of spines.

O. turpinii, sometimes considered as a variety of *O. diademata,* is a desirable plant, low and spreading in habit, with papery spines. The joints are thinner than those of *O. diademata*.

(c) *Opuntia*

Although these opuntias have flat plate-like stems, the young seedlings start with a cylindrical stem from which the flattened segments or 'pads' are produced. This would seem to indicate a cylindrical-stemmed ancestor. The new growth of each pad also carries minute awl-shaped leaves which soon shrivel and drop off.

The flat padded opuntias, or Prickly Pears, are usually amongst the first plants that appear in a cactus collection. They are also probably the first to go when the greenhouse or window-sill is full. One hastily looks round for some other 'innocent' who would like to accept a good flourishing cactus. The trouble is that the most vigorous opuntias are the ones most readily propagated and given away. These plants make magnificent specimens in a greenhouse large enough to accommodate bedded-out plants, and a 1·5 m. (5-ft.) specimen in full bloom is a spectacular sight. Besides, you can eat the fruit afterwards! There is, however, no need to grow *O. vulgaris*, other easily-tamed species exist, some of which will even weaken and die of neglect, like any 'normal' cactus. Occasionally one hears of an opuntia flowering regularly in a 15-cm. (6-in.) pot; these are the exception and opuntias should be grown for their beautiful spines and shapes.

The flat padded opuntias are the most widely distributed of all the cacti. Several species, including *O. fragilis* and *O. polyacantha* are found as far north as Canada where they grow in the drier parts of Alberta and British Columbia. Species of opuntia spread south through the United States and Mexico, right to the tip of the South American continent. They have also spread abroad. It is often difficult to persuade people that cacti are exclusively American after they have seen large specimens of *O. ficus-indica* growing along the Mediterranean coast. These plants have been introduced at some time in the past. Where the opuntia has really excelled itself is in Australia, a country with an ideal cactus climate, and no cactus enemies. The first opuntia, *O. monocantha*, was introduced in 1788, but made little progress. In 1839, some ardent cactophile introduced *O. inermis* to New South Wales. The pads broke off and were spread across the continent by wind and animals, until in 1920 150 million hectares (60 million acres) were covered with this plant, despite determined attacks with fire and poison to halt its progress. *O. monocantha* was exterminated by introducing the cochineal insect, but this did not attack the more rampant species. This was one of the first cases of biological control of a pest. The Australian Government commissioned research on natural pests of cacti and a South American moth, *Cactoblastic cactorum*, was found to have a caterpillar stage which lived on opuntia pads. This has been most useful in exterminating *O. inermis*.

Several flat-padded opuntias are almost hardy in the British Isles, particularly in the south. *O. cantabrigiensis* grows and flowers freely in the Botanic Garden at Cambridge. The British experience proves that, if one selects cacti with great care and foresight, with a weather eye upon the hazards, natural and otherwise that the plant will face, a cactus can be grown successfully almost anywhere.

In parts of America, opuntias are cultivated for their fruit, which is canned. Opuntia picking must be quite a hazardous occupation. Luther Burbank spent a great deal of time and money breeding a spineless opuntia for cattle food. He finally succeeded, but the cattle ate it so voraciously that the areas had to be replanted. However, the venture was not successful since the opuntia would only grow and flourish really well in regions of rainfall sufficient to grow more nutritious crops.

Opuntias should be generously potted and grown in a fairly rich compost. In the summer they can take a great deal of water, much like any other pot plant, and even in winter, they should not be allowed to dry out completely, otherwise some of the pads will shrivel and drop off. Some opuntias, particularly Mexican species such as *O. microdasys*, develop brown spots on their pads. This is due to cold, and if a temperature of above 7 °C (45 °F) can be maintained, this trouble will be eliminated.

O. basilaris is found in a region stretching from Northern Mexico into the United States. It is one of the most popular opuntias in cultivation due to its beautiful purplish-blue epidermis, and also because of its convenient size. As a pot plant it is not a vigorous grower, rarely being more than two pads tall, although in the wild, it is said to make a bush about 1 m. (3 ft.) high. The pads are oval with red glochids, and almost spineless. The flowers are red. There is a very attractive variety, *O. b.* var. *cordata*, which is much rarer; the pads are heart-shaped and branches only form at the base.

O. bergeriana is grown in the south of France as a flowering plant; pads with dark red flowers on them are sold in the markets. The country of origin is unknown. It is a tree-like plant with oval pads and yellow glochids. We planted a specimen of this opuntia in a trough, but were never able to flower it; others have been more successful.

O. dillenii is found along the coast of the south-eastern United States, and spreads into the West Indies, Mexico and S. America. It forms a large bush with very spiny pads. The flowers are pale yellow.

O. engelmannii occurs in the southern United States and Mexico. It makes a spreading bush with large joints. The numerous spines may be as much as 5 cm. (2 in.) long; the flowers are yellow.

O. ficus-indica is one opuntia cultivated for its fruit, and there are

61

a number of cultivated varieties with different coloured fruits, and fruits ripening at different times. As a pot plant it is not particularly attractive, having thin almost spineless pads of a greyish-green colour. If planted out in a large greenhouse, it will make a tree-like specimen and will flower. There is a variety with variegated pads.

O. herrfeldtii is an attractive small opuntia with almost circular pads. It is found in Central Mexico and needs a temperature of at least 7 °C (45 °F) if it is to be kept unmarked. The velvety pads are greyish-green in colour and spineless. They are neatly dotted all over with areoles containing red-brown glochids. The flowers are yellow.

O. leucotricha is found in Central Mexico, where it reaches tree-like proportions. The oval joints are covered with hair-like white spines, giving a very beautiful appearance. This plant needs a little extra warmth to be grown successfully, but it is certainly worth the effort. The flowers are deep yellow and the fruit is sold in the Mexican markets.

O. microdasys is one of the opuntias most frequently seen in cultivation. It is Mexican in origin and rather sensitive to low temperatures; if kept too cold, the pads develop red spots and a tendency to shrivel. It does occasionally flower as a pot plant; the flowers are pale yellow. The plant is much branched, with oval, spineless pads covered with prominent areoles containing yellow glochids. A number of horticultural varieties are known.

Var. *albispina* is the most beautiful of the *O. microdasys* varieties; it has silvery areoles and glochids.

Var. *minima* is a very small variety, the pads being about 5 cm. (2 in.) long compared to 12·5 or 13 cm. (5 or 6 in.) in the ordinary species.

Var. *pallida* has very pale yellow areoles and glochids.

Var. *rufida* has reddish-brown glochids. The plant is a darker green than the other varieties and the pads are shorter and thicker.

O. paraguayensis is a large padded plant and is somewhat easier to flower than many of the opuntias. The flowers are yellow.

O. phaeacantha is found in the southern United States and is fairly hardy. The almost circular joints have yellowish glochids and brown spines. The flowers are yellow.

O. polyacantha is a hardy opuntia which is widely distributed, being found in British Columbia and Alberta and spreading down the Western Coast of the United States. The joints are almost circular and quite attractively spined.

O. puberula is a Mexican species rather similar in appearance to *O. microdasys*. The pads are velvety, with bright yellow areoles and glochids.

O. rastrera is a hardy Mexican species with yellow areoles and beautiful spines. The flowers are yellow.

O. robusta is as its name implies, a vigorous plant. This makes it very useful as a source of grafting stock. The almost circular pads have an attractive bluish colour. The number of spines is variable. In its native Mexico a form of this tree-like plant is grown for fruit.

O. scheeri is a particularly beautiful species and it is not too vigorous. The whole surface of the oval pads is covered with a meshwork of golden spines. The flower colour, as usual, is yellow.

Grusonia

The last genus in the opuntia tribe is *Grusonia*; this forms an interesting link between *Opuntia* and *Cereus*. There is only one species, *G. bradtiana*. This is a plant up to 2 m. (6 ft.) in height with cylindrical ribbed joints. The tiny leaves soon shrivel. The glochids are found only on the young growth, and are shed as the stem matures. They are also found on the fruit. The flowers are yellow. We have grown *G. bradtiana*, but this native of Mexico does not seem to be quite so easy to cultivate as the opuntias. This plant is sometimes listed under its former name of *Opuntia cereiformis*.

FIVE

Giant Cacti

The average amateur is unable to show the giant cacti at their best, since a mature specimen in its native state is truly enormous. However, there is a fascination in a few pot specimens of these giants of the cactus world, and some are quite attractive as young plants, although they can never be considered as more than 'seedlings'.

The giants of the desert can be divided into two types; the columnar cerei, which often reach tree-like proportions, and the huge barrel cacti.

A very rare cactus, which, although not one of the largest specimens, seems to form a link between the jointed grusonias and the continuous columns of the cerei, is *Cereus ghiesbreghtii*. Globular or short cylindrical joints are piled one on top of the other to form a column. The joints are broadly ribbed and spiny. This is a very slow-growing plant and is seldom seen in cultivation. Another similar 'link' plant is *Arthrocereus microsphaericus*.

For every rarity there are many vigorous species which are rather dull, green columns. A large number of these are not in cultivation. They are too large for our greenhouses and their spines are not beautiful enough to make the young seedlings attractive as pot plants. However, they have uses. Some of the more common ones make excellent grafting stock.

The American continent is a large place, and as well as the hillsides covered with the common *Cereus jamacaru*, there are other slow-growing, highly coloured cacti to be found. Although eventually making huge specimens, they may take a hundred years to do so.

Giant Cacti

We shall deal with the large cerei first, and keep the huge, globular cacti together. There is much controversy about the naming of these plants; some botanists seem to have had a field day splitting large genera into smaller ones, whilst others have been equally busy re-combining them. We are on the side of simplicity, a few large genera rather than many splinter groups. We shall try to indicate which smaller genera have been joined together to form a composite one, so that if you meet a plant called *Loxanthocereus*, it will not be a complete mystery.

Armatocereus

These cacti are included in the *Lemairocereus* by some authorities. *Armatocereus cartwrightianus* makes a much branched plant about 4·5 m. (15 ft.) high. *A. godingianus* is tree-like with a woody trunk, reaching a height of about 12 m. (40 ft.). They are South American and rarely cultivated.

Carnegiea

The genus *Carnegiea* contains only one species, *C. gigantea*, the state flower of Arizona, often known as the Saguaro (pronounced Sah-*wah*-ro). The plant grows in south and west Arizona, north-west Mexico, and the northernmost section of Baja California, where it is found in stony deserts, and on rocky mountain slopes up to 1,100 m. (3,500 ft.). In Arizona there is a special reservation of 194,000 hectares (78,644 acres), the Saguaro National Monument. In this reservation there are well-marked footpaths and visitors can even hire horses from the local ranches to explore the area. *Carnegiea gigantea* is one of the largest cacti, and also one of the slowest-growing, taking about 10 years to produce a 15-cm. (6-in.) specimen. In 30 years the plant will be about 1 m. (39 in.) high. At 3 m. (10 ft.) it starts to branch; by then it is about 75 years old. A specimen of about 15 m. (50 ft.) in height and 2 m. (7 ft.) across is probably about two centuries old; it would then weigh about 6,000 kg. (6 tons). A well-grown specimen aged about a century has that characteristic shape of a

Giant Cacti

gigantic up-raised hand with which any enthusiast of Western films must be familiar.

The Saguaro blooms when about 40 years of age; the greenish-white flowers open around May to June and, as with many night-flowering cacti, they are fragrant.

Although seed must be produced in vast quantities in the Rincon Mountain section of the Saguaro National Monument, the plants are dying off and there are few seedlings to take their place. The cause of this is being investigated by the University of Arizona, but so far (1968), the exact cause of the disease is not known. In one area the number of plants has diminished from 1,400 in 1940 to 900 in 1965. One theory is that a disease is being spread by moths. Another is that the climate is not so favourable for the carnegieas as it was a couple of centuries ago. The Saguaro is very vulnerable despite, or because of, its immense size. Its shallow root system makes it unstable during heavy gales, and the enormous amount of water stored inside the plant means disaster if there should be a sudden frost. The lack of seedlings is probably explained by overgrazing by cattle, and the local rodents are probably not averse to a succulent seedling. Fortunately in other areas, such as the Sonora desert of Mexico and the Tucson Mountain area of the Saguaro National Monument, *C. gigantea* seems to be flourishing.

Cephalocereus

The genus *Cephalocereus* is one that has suffered greatly at the hands of the taxonomists. At one time it contained 68 species, but those with a pseudocephalium have now been placed in the genus *Pilosocereus*. Backeberg has created the genus *Austrocephalocereus* for the *Cephalocereus* species found in South America. The flowers of *Cephalocereus* and *Austrocephalocereus* are pollinated by vampire bats. Before going any further it is necessary to define the terms cephalium and pseudocephalium. A cephalium is a mass of hair which originates from the growing point of a cactus, and in which the flowers are formed. A pseudocephalium is derived from ordinary areoles which later develop hair.

Giant Cacti

Cephalocereus form enormous unbranched columns. The plants in *Austrocephalocereus* tend to branch from the ground, and are much smaller.

The most famous species is undoubtedly *Cephalocereus senilis*, the 'Old Man Cactus' from Mexico. In its native state, *C. senilis* forms columns up to 12 m. (40 ft.) high and about 45 cm. (18 in.) across. These plants are thought to be about 200 years old, so that there is no problem about growing the plant even in the smallest greenhouse.

Young specimens are pale green in colour, with slender yellow spines. From the areoles, 20 to 30 long white hairs are formed; these may be up to 12 cm. (5 in.) long in a well-grown plant. Unfortunately the hairs very soon lose their silvery appearance. Some books recommend shampooing the plant, and whilst this removes soot and mud from the hairs, a certain amount of the discoloration is due to irreversible chemical changes in the plant tissue. The only way to keep a perfect specimen is to cut the plant and re-root the young growth.

Very old specimens of *C. senilis* lose the hair completely, except for the top metre (39 in.) of the column. When about 6 m. (20 ft.) high the cactus develops a cephalium. The white flowers are nocturnal.

Cephalocereus senilis is found growing on hot, slaty cliffs and should be cultivated in an open compost, being kept dry in winter at a minimum temperature of 4–5 °C (40 °F).

Another species which may be met is *C. hoppenstedtii*, which eventually reaches a height of about 9 m. (30 ft.) in nature. While lacking the long hair of the previous species, this cactus has attractive white spines; it is also slow-growing.

The plants listed under *Austrocephalocereus* seem to be quite small cacti which should fit easily into a greenhouse collection.

A. dybowskii from Brazil and Bolivia is a freely-branching plant; in the native state the stems are about 3·5 m. (12 ft.) high, 8 cm. (3 in.) thick, and covered with silky white hairs.

A. lehmannianus, also from Brazil, makes a branching plant about 2 m. (6 ft.) high and 8 cm. (3 in.) thick. The stem is a bluish colour with woolly aeroles and covered with dense white spines. These are both tropical plants and need a winter temperature of about 10 °C (50 °F).

Giant Cacti

Cereus

At one time every cactus that was not an opuntia, and was not globular, was called a cereus. There were at least 300 of them; now only plants belonging to the same group as the original type species, *Cereus hexagonus*, are included. There are about 26 species.

Young plants of cerei are straight columns, but with age they form a candelabra-like crown, whilst some species branch from the base; these are the so-called 'Organ Cacti'. All have large, nocturnal flowers, usually white or pink. They are vigorous growers, and useful as grafting stock. If planted in the border of a large greenhouse, or bedded out in summer, some species will flower in cultivation.

Cerei are South American in origin, and hillsides are covered with groves of these cacti. In cultivation they are easy, almost too easy. They are so vigorous that they quickly outgrow their accommodation. Despite their tropical origin, they are quite tough and a minimum winter temperature of about 5 °C (41 °F) is sufficient.

C. argentinensis is true to its name, coming from Argentina. It is a large plant, reaching a height of 12 m. (40 ft.) and much branched.

C. coerulescens is a slender bluish column, found in Argentina. This species flowers when young; the funnel-shaped flowers are 20 cm. (8 in.) long.

C. hexagonus is a column up to about 9 m. (30 ft.) high and 15 cm. (6 in.) thick. The blue to grey-green stems branch freely in nature. It is found in areas of South America.

C. jamacaru and the rather similar *C. peruvianus* are frequently met in cultivation. They are the cerei that invariably turn up in packets of mixed cactus seed. Fortunately, the young plants make excellent grafting stock. Both plants are much-branched in the natural habitat, but seldom do so in collections, unless deliberately beheaded. In the wild state, these cacti eventually make a height of 9 m. (30 ft.) and the stems are bluish-green in colour. Both these cacti come from South America, *C. peruvianus* in particular from Brazil and north Argentina. *C. repandus*, from tropical America, is another plant which makes a good 9 m. (30 ft.) in height, and branches freely.

68

Jasminocereus

This plant with the delightful name is seldom met in cultivation. It is a tree-like cereus with a much-branched head, and the flowers smell strongly of jasmine. There is only one species, named after its homeland, *Jasminocereus galapagensis*. It comes from the Galapagos Islands, Ecuador.

Lemaireocereus

Lemaireocereus forms a convenient umbrella to cover many smaller 'genera' whose status seems somewhat uncertain, namely *Hertrichocereus, Isolatocereus, Marginatocereus, Neolemairocereus, Polaskia, Ritterocereus,* and *Stenocereus.* These plants are widely spread from Arizona through Mexico down to Cuba, Venezuela and Peru. The North American species are the easiest; the tropical ones need a high winter temperature.

In appearance, lemaireocerei form tall columns, branching from just above the ground. The small flowers are whitish in colour and open during the day.

L. beneckii comes from Central Mexico where it may grow up to 3 m. (10 ft.) in height and 9 cm. (3½ in.) thick. It has few branches and a thick powdery bloom covers the stem. There are about 5 stiff radial spines, up to 4 cm. (1½ in.) long and 1 central. These start red in colour and pass to grey. This is one of the most beautiful lemaireocerei, but rather difficult to cultivate, needing a higher winter temperature than most. It is probably better grafted.

L. chichipe is a Mexican species, reaching a height of about 4·5 m. (15 ft.). The young spines are a reddish colour. The seedlings are attractive, being covered with a powdery meal, and they are slow-growing.

L. dumortieri comes from Central Mexico and needs to be kept warm and dry. The stem reaches a height of 9 m. (30 ft.) or more and the very prominent ribs carry needle-like white spines. It has a noticeable 'bloom'.

L. marginatus is used as a hedging plant in Mexico where it forms a branching column up to 6 m. (20 ft.) high. It is a beautiful and fast-growing species. The spines are small and stiff. This plant is quite easy to grow, but prefers a winter temperature of at least 7 °C (45 °F).

L. thurberi occurs as far north as Arizona and continues down into Mexico. The plant branches freely from the base and will eventually reach a height of over 6 m. (20 ft.). The stems are purplish-green with glossy black spines on the new growth. The white flowers are followed by edible fruit. The attractive seedlings are slow-growing.

L. weberi is a Mexican species which reaches a height of 9 m. (30 ft.). This cactus forms very few basal shoots, but branches freely from the head. The stem is a bluish-green colour.

Neobuxbaumia

These are large, many-ribbed, columnar cacti which do not branch freely. They are found in the hot gulleys of Mexico. The species most commonly met is *Neobuxbaumia polylopha* which is slow-growing and makes an attractive pot plant, although in its native country it makes a column about 15 m. (50 ft.) high and 75 cm. (2½ ft.) across. The stem is divided into about 30 ribs; the bell-shaped flowers are dark red. Rather similar species are *N. tetetzo* and *N. euphorbioides*. All need a somewhat higher winter temperature than most cacti; at least 7 °C (45 °F). *N. polylopha* grows out of doors in the Jardin Exotique, Monaco.

Pachycereus

This genus includes a number of vast, tree-like cacti, some of which are even larger than *Carnegiea gigantea*. The rather small flowers open in daytime. Cuttings are by no means easy to root, making it difficult to keep a specimen within bounds by re-rooting the young growth. They can, however, be grafted.

Pachycereus pecten-arboriginum has its main claim to fame because pieces of spiny rib and the spiny fruits are said to be used by the natives as combs. It is a branching plant about 9 m. (30 ft.) high and 1 m. (3 ft.) across at the base, found in Mexico.

P. pringlei (elephant cactus) is often met in cultivation. This Mexican cactus will reach a height of around 12 m. (40 ft.). The seedlings make attractive columns for the back of the greenhouse staging. The greyish stem carries many black-brown spines. Plants in the wild start branching at about 1 m. (39 in.) from the ground.

Pilosocereus

The name *Pilosocereus* is quite a recent one, being proposed by Byles and Rowley in 1957 to replace *Pilocereus, Lem*. The name *Pilocereus* was considered untenable because it was based on the same type species as *Cephalocereus (C. senilis)*. To complicate matters further, another botanist, Schumann, had also included plants in a genus *Pilocereus*. *Pilosocereus* includes *Pilocereus, K. Schum.*, and some plants which were formerly included in *Cephalocereus* and *Cereus*. They need a minimum winter temperature of about 7 °C (45 °F).

The species most often met is *Pilosocereus palmeri*, still often listed under its old name *Cephalocereus palmeri*. This is a branching column, about 4·5 m. (15 ft.) high, coming from the warm valleys of eastern Mexico. The areoles produce long white hairs which are very prominent on the flowering side of the stem, forming a pseudocephalium. The nocturnal flowers are pink.

Other species include *P. moritzianus* from Venezuela, which makes about 9 m. (30 ft.), and *P. glaucescens*, a Brazilian species of about 6 m. (20 ft.) with pale blue stems.

Stetsonia

There is only one species of *Stetsonia*, the very beautiful *S. coryne*. The seedlings make the most delightful pot plants, with their long spines, changing from white to black with age. The seedlings are slow-growing; in our experience they are also difficult to keep. We have never had the embarrassment of a stetsonia trying to lift the greenhouse roof off.

In their native Argentina, stetsonias make tree-like plants about 7·5 m. (25 ft.) high. The flowers are white.

BARREL CACTI

Although the tree-like cerei form an impressive part of the desert landscape, they are not the only large cacti. Some of the 'barrels' reach a gigantic size and must weigh close on 1,000 kg. (1 ton).

Giant Cacti

Echinocactus

At one time all cacti which were globular in shape and therefore not cerei, were called *Echinocactus*. Like the cerei, the echinocacti have been pruned and the genus has been reduced to about nine species.

Echinocacti are found in Mexico and the south-west states of the United States, where they bake in the full sun of the desert. Two species, *Echinocactus horizonthalonius* and *E. polycephalus*, are difficult to grow in cultivation. They need a higher temperature than most, and are extra sensitive to stagnant moisture. The other species are easy to grow and require a minimum winter temperature of about 5 °C (41 °F). All species like full sunshine; it is very difficult to flower even mature specimens in any climate with low light intensity.

The echinocactus family is characterised by heavily-spined, barrel-shaped plants, for the most part. Flowers are found near the crown of mature specimens. The flowers of echinocacti form a ring around the top of the plant.

E. grandis is found in Mexico, where it forms a plant about 1 m. (39 in.) in diameter and 2 m. (6 ft.) high. It has about 40 ribs, carrying brown spines. The small yellow flowers are embedded in the woolly top.

E. grusonii, the 'Golden Barrel', is found in the deserts of Central Mexico, and there are few large collections which have not at least one specimen. This cactus is very easily raised from seed; the seedlings have tubercles and look like golden mammillarias. It is not until they are several years old that they develop the characteristic ribs of the adult plant, about 28 in number. *E. grusonii* is found in the deserts of Central Mexico. It is almost globular, reaching a diameter of about 1 m. (39 in.), but these plants must be extremely old, for in cultivation this cactus takes about 10 years to reach a diameter of 15 cm. (6 in.). The awl-shaped spines are a pale golden-yellow, and there is deep golden wool on the crown of the plant. The small flowers are yellow.

E. horizonthalonius is not an easy plant to obtain. Occasionally some imported specimens appear on the market, but they are difficult to re-establish. This echinocactus has a wide distribution, Mexico, New Mexico, Texas, and Arizona. It is a flattened plant, up to 30 cm. (12 in.) across at maturity; it must be the 'baby' of the genus. The stem is bluish-green in colour, with thick greyish spines, and divided into 7–13 ribs. The flowers are pink. This is the one species that can be flowered in cultivation, provided it can be kept alive long enough!

E. ingens is an enormous plant about 1·5 m. (5 ft.) high and across, divided into about 55 ribs. It is greyish-green with stiff brown spines and the small yellow flowers are produced on the very woolly top. It comes from Mexico. It is easy to grow.

E. polycephalus is found in southern California, Mexico, Arizona, Nevada and Utah. Like the other widely distributed plant, *E. horizonthalonius*, it is not easy to cultivate. It is a cylindrical plant, about 25 cm. (10 in.) across and 1 m. (39 in.) high, branching to form large groups. The spines are brown. As with the other species, the yellow flowers are produced from the woolly crowns of the plants. In its native homeland, it grows amongst boulders and gravel where the roots spread far out in search of moisture. It is very sensitive to bad drainage, and needs plenty of root room.

Eriosyce

The 'Giant Balls' of the Cordilleras are large, solitary cacti which can reach a height of about 1 m. (39 in.) and a diameter up to 30 cm. (1 ft.). They need a well-drained soil and as much sun as we can give them.

E. aurata bears a resemblance to *Echinocactus grusonii*, being about the same size and with roughly the same number of ribs and golden-yellow spines. It is found in Chile.

E. ceratites, also from Chile, has about 35 ribs equipped with numerous awl-shaped spines. These are yellow on the new growth, but turn brown with age. The red bell-shaped flowers are carried near the top of the plant.

Ferocactus

The name *Ferocactus* means 'ferocious cactus', and this describes the spines very aptly. These plants, with their fierce, beautifully coloured spines, are found in Arizona, California, Texas and Mexico. The large species tend to be solitary, the smaller ones cluster. The flowers are borne on top of the plant. Although giants in nature, ferocacti are slow-growing, and are quite commonly seen in collections, but we have found that they need rather more care than many cacti; they need as much sun as possible and watering cautiously.

F. acanthodes is found in southern California where it makes a cylindrical plant about 3 m. (9 ft.) high and 1 m. (39 in.) across. It has about 23 ribs and the spines are of a beautiful reddish colour. The flowers are yellow or orange and about 5 cm. (2 in.) long.

F. covillei from Arizona, reaches a height of about 1·5 m. (5 ft.) and has red spines. The flowers are either red or yellow.

F. johnstonianus is a very rare species from Baja California, on the Angel de la Guardia Island which has a climate of such heat and drought that the giant cacti of the mainland are stunted dwarfs. *F. johnstonianus* is found amongst the rocks of this island. It is a sphere or short column, covered in brilliant yellow spines; the flowers are pale yellow; on removal to any damper climate, the spines lose their brilliant colour.

F. latispinus (syn. *F. corniger*) occurs in Mexico at about 3,000 m. (10,000 ft.) above sea level. It is a plant about 30 cm. (1 ft.) high and has red spines. The flowers are mauve.

F. melocactiformis (syn. *F. electroacanthus*) forms a clustering plant in its native Mexico. The stems make a height of about 60 cm. (2 ft.) and have yellow spines. The flowers are yellow.

F. wislizenii occurs in Texas, Mexico and Arizona, where it makes a column about 2 m. (6 ft.) high and 1 m. (39 in.) across. The spines and flowers are yellowish.

Soehrensia

The *Soehrensia*, or 'giant lobivia', were once included in the genus *Lobivia*, to which they are related. They require the same conditions as lobivias, namely full sun in summer, and a cool, dry winter rest. They are easily raised from seed, but are slow-growing. *S. bruchii* is the type species. This is a globular plant with about 50 ribs, furnished with stout spines, and when mature, reaches a height of about 1·2 m. (4 ft.). The flowers are red. Argentina is the homeland of this cactus.

Other species are the yellow-flowered *S. ferox* with very long, slender spines, and *S. schaeferi*, also very long-spined.

SIX

Large Cacti

There are a large number of cacti which reach a height of from 60 cm. to 3 m. (2 to 10 ft.) in nature; these species may not have the majestic appearance of a giant *Pachycereus*, but they look impressive when planted out in the bed of a large greenhouse. Many of these will flower in northern climes and thrive as pot plants for many years. We have seen a specimen of *Cleistocactus strausii* flowering in the size of pot that would house a tomato plant, and it certainly took up no more space than a fruiting tomato. So it is possible for the owner of even a small green-house to grow one or two tall columnar plants. In addition, there are some large, globular cacti with stout spines which make an attractive addition to a collection.

The distinction between 'giant' and 'large' cacti is purely arbitrary, and we have used it in reference to the ultimate size in their native habitat. However, few, if any, collectors can grow any of these plants to their native size, so from the cultivation angle the separation is less obvious. Indeed, in a collection, a 'large' cactus may be bigger than a 'giant'. However, in this section we shall deal with plants which, although attaining a size in nature greater than we are likely to see in our greenhouses, nevertheless do not reach the dimensions of the real giants.

Arequipa

These plants are native to Chile and Peru, and are named after the city of Arequipa in Peru, in the neighbourhood of which *A. leucotricha* was found. This is a small genus containing *A. clavata*, *A. hempeliana*, *A. leucotricha* and *A. weingartiana*. The stems are

Large Cacti

many-ribbed, and the large, carmine, oblique flowers are carried at the top.

The most commonly cultivated species is *A. leucotricha*. We have found this easy to raise from seed, but slow-growing. The cylindrical stem eventually makes a height of about 60 cm. (2 ft.), and is about 10 cm. (4 in.) thick. The stem is greyish-green in colour and covered with yellow spines.

Arrojadoa

These Brazilian cacti, closely related to *Cephalocereus*, are not often cultivated. The slender stems can reach a length of about 2 m. (6 ft.) and a pseudocephalium develops at the top of the stem from which the flowers appear; these are violet-red in colour.

Borzicactus

Some botanists use the genus *Borzicactus* as a sort of umbrella covering a multitude of 'genera': *Bolivicereus, Clistanthocereus, Loxanthocereus, Maritimocereus*, and *Seticereus*. The plants are found in Bolivia, Ecuador, and Peru. Although they occur as high as 2,500 m. (8,000 ft.) above sea level, in these equatorial regions the temperature never drops very low. One grower has suggested a minimum temperature of 13 °C (55 °F) both summer and winter. This makes the plants difficult to keep as they are not of a size that can be put into the propagator for the winter. Many species have a decumbent habit, which is space consuming. However, they flower when young; the flowers are about 5 cm. (2 in.) across and are mainly in shades of red and orange. Draughts or a sudden drop in temperature must be avoided, otherwise the buds will probably shrivel. The slender, branching stems may be columnar or prostrate, and often have beautifully coloured spines. *Borzicactus acanthurus* has prostrate stems about 30 cm. (1 ft.) long and covered with yellow spines. It is found in Peru at altitudes of over 2,300 m. (7,500 ft.).

B. gracilis is a prostrate plant with golden-yellow spines, and brilliant orange flowers.

Large Cacti

B. icosagonus from Ecuador is an erect plant, about 15 m. (5 ft.) high in the wild. It is covered with numerous golden-yellow spines.

This genus now includes the plant known as *Hildewintera auriespina*, syn. *Winterocereus auriespina*. *Borzicactus auriespina*, as we should now call it, is found in the foothills of the Andes, where it grows on sheer sandstone cliffs, with the stems hanging down the rock face. It is a fast-growing plant, with golden-yellow spines. Specimens about 40 cm. (16 in.) in length have been flowered; the flowers are salmon-pink.

Cleistocactus

There must be very few collections which have not at one time contained a specimen of *Cleistocactus strausii*. This silvery column is one of many choice cacti found in the genus. Cleistocacti are slender, columnar plants which branch from the base. They will flower in cultivation, but are usually about 1·5 m. (5 ft.) tall before doing so. The flowers are very characteristic, consisting of a long, narrow tube which is almost closed. The opening is only large enough for the stamens to protrude. Cleistocactus means 'closed cactus', referring to these flowers. The flowers are borne on the sides of the columns.

These South American plants are very easily raised from seed, and grow vigorously. We have found that *C. strausii* and *C. baumannii* make excellent grafting stock. They will withstand some frost if kept completely dry.

C. baumannii is a slender plant, about 4 cm. (1½ in.) thick and reaches a height of 2 m. (6 ft.), and therefore tends to need some support. It is covered with dark brown spines, up to about 2·5 cm. (1 in.) long. The flowers are orange-scarlet and with an 'S' shape, instead of the usual straight tube. The plant is found in Argentina, Uruguay and Paraguay.

C. buchtienii is a vigorous plant with golden-brown spines and bright red flowers. The stems are stiff and will reach a height of about 2 m. (6 ft.).

C. luribayensis has honey-coloured central spines which may reach a length of 8 cm. (3 in.). The flowers are reddish-pink.

C. morawetzianus is a yellow-spined species from Peru. It has stems over 5 cm. (2 in.) thick, and reaching a height of 2 m. (6 ft.). So far it is the only known species with white flowers.

C. ritteri is a white hairy plant with lemon-coloured flowers. Another species with dense, almost white spines is unnamed, but is known in the trade as *C. de Santa Cruz*, meaning 'from Santa Cruz'. It has flowers which deepen from orange through to scarlet.

C. strausii is the best-known silvery species. This Bolivian cactus has stems up to 1·5 m. (5 ft.) high, which branch from the base, and are covered with short white spines. The flowers are carmine.

Corryocactus

Corryocactus are South American plants with columnar stems, branching from the base, and are very spiny. The flowers are large and yellowish or reddish in colour. We find that these cacti make excellent grafting stock. *C. brachypetalus* and *C. brevistylus* are plants which freely branch from the base and would in nature make a height of around 3 m. (10 ft.). The stems are about 5 cm. (2 in.) thick and covered with dark brown spines. They are found in Chile and Peru.

C. melanotrichus is a smaller plant from Bolivia, which may reach a height of 2m. (6 ft.) and has yellowish spines.

Denmoza

Denmoza is an anagram of Mendoza, a town in Argentina near which the first specimens were found. These plants are related to *Cleistocactus*, and have the same long, tubular flowers of that genus. The red flowers are carried on top of the plant. There are two species.

D. erythrocephala is a solitary plant which is about 1·2 m. (4½ ft.) high when mature. The spines are also reddish, but more numerous than in the previous species.

D. rhodacantha is a globular plant, becoming cylindrical with age. It sprouts from the base. The stem is dark green in colour with many ribs, equipped with long reddish spines.

Large Cacti

Erdisia

Erdisia is a small genus from Peru and Chile. The plants have large, swollen roots and slender branching stems with few ribs. The flowers are small and bell-shaped. *E. mayenii* is a yellow-flowered species with underground, spineless stems. *E. spiniflora* is similar, but with purple flowers.

E. squarrosa with stems up to 2 in. (6 ft.) long and 4 cm. (1½ in.) thick is the largest species. It has long, yellowish spines, and red flowers, about 5 cm. (2 in.) long, on the ends of the branches. Other species are *E. philippii, E. erecta* and *E. quadrangularis.*

Escontria

Escontria are tree-like plants with short, thick, much-branched stems, divided into 7 or 8 ribs. They have short yellowish spines and small yellow flowers.

E. chiotilla is found in Mexico, and is named after the native name for the edible fruits, 'chiotilla'.

Espostoa

These are branching cacti which sometimes reach a height of 3.5 m. (12 ft.). They have many ribs and numerous spines, as well as a great deal of silvery hair. The small, reddish flowers are produced from a cephalium. *Espostoa* are found in Peru and Ecuador. In our experience, they are not easy to keep, rotting readily at the base, but we have a damp winter to contend with.

E. lanata is a columnar plant, completely covered with white silky wool. *E. melanostele* also has white hair, but the yellow spines protrude through. As with other hairy cacti, the most beautiful silk is on the new growth. The hair on the lower stems darkens and often wears off. The only cure for this is to cut off the top, dry very thoroughly, and re-root.

Eulychnia

Eulychnia are found in Chile, where they make shrubby plants ultimately reaching a height of about 3·5 m. (12 ft.).

The species most often seen in cultivation is *E. acida*. This is a

Trichocereus glottsbergii

Ancistrocactus scheeri. A young specimen

Astrophytum myriostigma

*Dolichothele
longimamma*

*Echinocereus
pentalophus*

Mammillaria brauneana. A large specimen, showing buds and seed-pods

*Mammillaria
longiflora*

*Mammillaria
microhelia*

Mammillaria zeilmanniana

Thelocactus bicolor

Chamaecereus silvestrii

Copiapoa cinerea

*Echinopsis
rhodotricha*

Echinobivia
'Green Gold'

*Gymnocalycium
andreae*

*Gymnocalycium
baldianum*

Gymnocalycium damsii

Gymnocalycium platense

Islaya brevicylindrica

Lobivia allegraiana (*hertrichiana* group)

Matucana aurantiaca

Neoporteria densispina

Notocactus 'apricus complex'

Notocactus graessneri

Notocactus leninghausii

Notocactus mammulosus

Parodia echinus

shrub with many long spines, the centrals reaching a length of up to 20 cm. (8 in.). This of course refers to a specimen in the wild; although lengths of 15 cm. (6 in.) have been quoted for specimens grown in this country, this type of growth is obtained only in very favoured regions. The small pink flowers are followed by juicy and slightly acid fruits.

E. spinibarbis is another long-spined species, with white flowers, followed by acid fruits.

Facheiroa

These Brazilian cacti produce their flowers from a cephalium. They are columnar plants with slender, branched stems. The type species, *F. ulei*, reaches a height of about 4·5 m. (15 ft.). The short spines are brown, the flowers small and white. Recently Ritter has discovered a second species which he has provisionally named *F. pilosa*. This latter has more ribs and shorter hair on the cephalium than *F. ulei*.

Haageocereus

The genus *Haageocereus* includes *Peruvocereus* and *Neobinghamia*. They are found on the Pacific coast of the Peruvian Andes, growing on dry cliffs. It is suggested by Borg that this region was once much damper than it is now. Hence the haageocerei can survive damp climates and they are not generally difficult in cultivation.

This genus consists of many-ribbed, columnar cacti, closely covered with brightly coloured spines. They are grown mainly for these spines, but have certainly been flowered in this country, including *Haageocereus decumbens* and its variety *multicolorispinus*, and *H. acranthus*. These plants need a free root run, and are seen at their best when planted out in a bed.

H. acranthus is a tall clustering plant, covered with yellow spines. The flowers are greenish-white and open fully at night. Other yellow-spined species are *H. chosicensis, H. comosus, H. laredensis, H. marksianus, H. pacalaensis* and *H. zehnderi*.

H. decumbens is a semi-prostrate plant with snowy-white spines. The sweetly-scented flowers are nocturnal. Two other white-spined species are *H. seticeps* and *H. pseudomelanostele*.

Large Cacti

Among the brown-spined species is *H. olowinskianus*. *H. versicolor* has yellow spines, with zones of reddish-brown ones.

Homalocephala

H. texensis is the only representative of this genus and is widely spread over Texas, New Mexico and Mexico. It is known as the 'Devil's Head' because of the stout spines capable of crippling a horse. The plant is so tough that it can survive being trodden on by a horse, with barely a dent. The plant is solitary and reaches a diameter of up to 30 cm. (1 ft.). It grows on open, sandy hills under a fierce sun. Often the top of *H. texensis* is flush with the surface of the soil; this gives the plant some protection from the heat. The ribs of this cactus are very prominent and equipped with formidable spines. These are dark red on the young growth, but turn grey with age. The fragrant flowers are deep pink in colour and last for several days. They are carried on top of the plant and are followed by bright pink seed-pods.

Lophocereus

Four species of *Lophocereus* have been described, *L. australis*, *L. gatesii*, *L. sargentianus*, and *L. schottii*, but Borg considers the first three to be varieties of *L. schottii*. This last species has an interesting monstrous form which we have included in the chapter on these plants. The first three species are found only in Baja California, but *L. schottii* occurs occasionally in Arizona. Lophocerei grow at the bottoms of sandy canyons and in cultivation need rich soil and plenty of water. These cacti are columnar plants which branch from the base to form clumps, and may reach a height of from 1 to 4·5 m. (3 to 15 ft.). The flowers are nocturnal and about 3 cm. (1¼ in.) long, varying in colour from white through pink to red. They are pollinated by moths which lay their eggs at the base of the areoles on the tips of the stems. The grubs eat out a gourd-shaped cavity which becomes lined with scar tissue. The fruit is bright scarlet.

The stems of the lophocerei are interesting; the lower parts have short stout spines, whilst the upper sections of the taller branches are covered with long weak spines. It is amongst these upper spines that the flowering areoles are found.

L. schottii is the stoutest species, with stems 20 cm. (8 in.) across, reaching a height of 5·5 m. (15 ft.). A good specimen may have as much as 25 branches. The monstrous variety is described in Chapter 11.

L. sargentianus is very similar in habit, except that the branches are more slender and numerous.

L. australis is the only species with a definite trunk. This plant can reach a height of 7·5 m. (25 ft.) and has hundreds of very slender branches arising from a short main stem.

L. gatesii is only about 3 m. (10 ft.) in height and the ribs are so closely spaced that the stems appear cylindrical, rather than angular as in the other species. The flowering stems are very densely covered with interlocking hairy spines.

Machaerocereus

There are two species of *Machaerocereus*, both found on remote islands of Baja California.

M. eruca, the 'Creeping Devil Cactus', has heavy prostrate stems equipped with whitish, dagger-like spines. It looks rather like a gigantic armed caterpillar creeping slowly across the desert. This is not altogether fanciful, the plant *is* creeping forward. The rear slowly dies off, whilst the newer sections of the stems take root. The tips are turned upwards and this enables the plant to pass over any stones or small rocks that are in its way. The stems act as sand binders. The creamish flowers are nocturnal.

We have seen *M. eruca* growing well in a greenhouse. It was planted in a narrow box, nearly a metre (3 ft.) long, so that the prostrate stem could root. For anyone with the space to spare (and if you can obtain a specimen), *M. eruca* needs a sandy soil, and a sunny position. Cuttings root easily.

M. gummosus has an upright habit and reaches a height of 2·5 m. (8 ft.). It spreads by layering. Long horizontal shoots bend over, root and start new colonies some distance away from the parent plant. The fruit of this cactus is edible, and the pulp from the stem contains a narcotic which is used to render the local fish unconscious; one way of catching fish without exerting too much effort. The flowers of this species are purplish-red.

Large Cacti

Melocactus

The 'Melon Thistle', or 'Turk's-cap', was one of the first cacti to be brought back alive to Europe by the early explorers. Illustrations of *Melocactus* appeared in herbals at the beginning of the 16th century. They are found growing in saline, sandy soil near the coast of tropical North and South America, as well as the West Indies. Melocacti have a need for a minimum winter temperature of about 15 °C (60 °F). There are about 30 species, but the plants are very variable and it is not always easy to distinguish distinct species. In appearance melocacti are globular or shortly-cylindrical plants. Mature specimens develop a cephalium from which the small pink flowers are produced. Some species reach a height of about 1 m. (39 in.), and all have pronounced ribs with stout spines. They have very shallow but widespread root systems; a plant the size of an orange may well have roots 3 m. (10 ft.) long. This is one of the reasons that they are difficult as greenhouse plants; it is almost impossible to give them the free root-run they need. The least difficult plant to cultivate is said to be *M. neryi* from Central Brazil; this is the only species found any distance from the sea. Another species sometimes seen in large collections is *M. communis*, from Jamaica.

Morawetzia

There is probably only one species of *Morawetzia*, *M. doelziana*, although the Zürich collection includes an *M. sericata*, attributed to Ritter. *M. doelziana* is very closely related to *Oreocereus*, but differing in forming a cephalium on the ends of the flowering shoots. The flowers are carmine. This cactus is found on the eastern slopes of the Andes, in Peru. The slender stems branch from the base and reach a height of about 1·5 m. (5 ft.). The numerous spines are reddish on the young growth, but turn grey with time. The spines are initially surrounded by white hairs, but these disappear as the stem ages. The plant is easy to cultivate and should be given the same treatment as oreocerei.

Large Cacti

Myrtillocactus

The name *Myrtillocactus* is derived from *myrtus*, the Latin name for myrtle. The berries of this cactus, resembling those of the latter, are edible and are sold in the Mexican markets.

Myrtillocacti are found in Mexico, California and Guatemala. To grow these plants successfully they need a winter temperature of about 13 °C (55 °F). *M. geometrizans* is a much-favoured grafting stock, particularly for the red *Gymnocalycium mihanovichii* 'Hibotan'. If you live in a cold area and buy a plant on this stock, take it off and re-graft on, say, a trichocereus. You may get away with it on the myrtillocactus stock for one winter, but sooner or later the stock will succumb to the cold, and will rot. If you are lucky your scion will be unaffected, but the middle of January is not the best time either to re-root or re-graft a rare plant.

The myrtillocactus most frequently offered for sale is *M. geometrizans*. This is found in Mexico and Guatemala, where it is used as a hedging plant. It reaches a height of about 3 m. (10 ft.) and forms many branches on a short trunk; these are of a beautiful bluish colour. In cultivation, these cacti do not branch freely, and rarely flower. Also the spines of pot-grown specimens are weak. The tiny white flowers, borne in clusters, are sweetly scented.

Four other species, *M. cochal, M. eichlamii, M. pugionifer,* and *M. schenckei*, are recognised by some.

Oreocereus

The *Oreocereus* are found on the eastern slopes of the Andes at altitudes of over 3,000 m. (10,000 ft.). At this height they are exposed to temperatures well below freezing, and we have found that if these cacti are kept completely dry during the winter, they are hardy. The stems are covered with varying amounts of white, silky hair, and branch freely from the base, forming clumps. As with other 'woolly' cacti, the lower parts of the stems become shabby with age. The flowers are small and red.

O. celsianus reaches a height of about 1 m. (39 in.) in cultivation.

Large Cacti

The yellowish-brown spines can be felt through the long, silky, white hairs.

O. fossulatus is less hairy than the above species, and has long, brownish spines. In cultivation, there is considerable variation in the amount of hair produced. Some growers claim that grafting is a cure for 'baldness'. Personally, we can think of no reason for grafting a plant which grows so well on its own roots, even at the expense of hair. As a general rule, lack of hair and spines on cacti under the conditions of cultivation is due to insufficient light in our climate, and there is little we can do about that.

O. hendriksenianus has long yellow hairs and reddish spines. The stems make a height of about 45 cm. (18 in.).

O. ritteri is a comparative newcomer, with abundant white wool and yellow spines. It grows well from seed, soon making a slim column.

O. trollii, the 'Old Man of the Andes', is a slow-growing species, eventually making a height of 1 m. (39 in.). The stem is covered with greyish-white wool, in which are embedded whitish spines.

Rathbunia

Rathbunia are straggling bushes, native to Mexico. They are found in very hot, dry localities.

R. alamosensis is a fast-growing bush, about 3.5 m. (12 ft.) high and with red flowers.

R. kerberi is about half the size of the above species and has pink flowers.

R. sonorensis and *R. pseudosonorensis* are the other two species. They are low-growing bushes, about 60 cm. (2 ft.) high with red flowers.

Stephanocereus

S. leucostele is a columnar plant, about 3 m. (10 ft.) high, found in Brazil. The spines are whitish and mature specimens bear a white cephalium. The nocturnal flowers are white. This is a vigorous growing plant, requiring full sun.

Large Cacti

Thrixanthocereus

These are columnar plants from the Andes. There are two species most likely to be met; they are both easy to grow, and as young plants are very beautiful.

T. blossfeldiorum is usually unbranched but occasionally branches from the base. It is particularly attractive, with pale radial spines and longer centrals, brown and black. Whitish flowers are formed from a pseudocephalium, on large specimens. This cactus comes from north Peru.

T. senilis is similar but covered with glistening white spines.

Some taxonomists classify *Thrixanthocereus* with *Facheiroa*, and in the Zürich catalogue both are included in *Espostoa*.

Trichocereus

Trichocereus have a particular claim to fame, they make good grafting stock, possibly the best. This tends to overshadow the fact that many of these cacti are attractive plants in their own right. They are columnar, branching from the base, and forming large clumps. A few species branch from above ground level, giving a candelabra-like effect. They all have large, bell-shaped flowers, and good-sized specimens will flower in cultivation, particularly if bedded out. They are native to the Andes, often growing at high altitudes.

T. bridgesii is a species from Bolivia, where it is used for hedging. The greyish-green stems reach a height of 4·5 m. (15 ft.) and have very long yellow spines. The large white flowers are sweetly scented.

T. candicans is found in Argentina, where it reaches a height of about 1 m. (39 in.). It forms enormous clumps; the stems are clad with long yellow spines and the scented flowers are white.

T. glottsbergii. This plant is often offered for sale, and makes a most attractive small specimen. The pale brown spines are long and stout, making it rather unsuitable for grafting stock, but it is well worth acquiring for its own sake.

T. macrogonus grows in both Bolivia and Argentina, making a height of 3 m. (10 ft.). The bluish-green stems have short brown spines, making the plant useful for grafting; long spines make this operation more difficult, and usually have to be cut away. The flowers are white.

T. pachanoi comes from Ecuador and Peru. It is a tall species, reaching up to 6 m. (20 ft.). Being often almost spineless in cultivation, it is an excellent grafting stock. It has scented white flowers.

T. schikendantzii is Argentinean. This is a smaller species about 1 m. (39 in.) high. The large white flowers are heavily scented. This is yet another short-spined species suitable for grafting.

T. spachianus, also from Argentina, is possibly the species most often used for grafting, for which its short spines make it very suitable. In its native land it reaches a height of about 1·5 m. (5 ft.). Again, the flowers are white.

T. terscheckii is an enormous species from Argentina, where it can reach 12 m. (40 ft.). It has strong yellow spines and white flowers.

T. thelogonus is a sprawling species, and in its native Argentina, the stems reach a length of about 1·5 m. (5 ft.). The large flowers are white.

Weberbauerocereus

These cacti are included under *Trichocereus* by Buxbaum.

Winterocereus

Now included under *Borzicactus*.

Zehntnerella

Z. squamulosa is native to Brazil, where it reaches a height of about 60 cm. (2 ft.). It branches from the base and the spiny stems carry small white flowers.

SEVEN

Cacti of North America

Most of us who grow cacti begin to hunt for buds as soon as the days start lengthening. With the large-growing species of the preceding chapters the chances of flowers in a small greenhouse are not very high. But the small, low-growing species will give a colourful display every summer.

Personally we think that the best flowering cacti come from South America (mammillaria enthusiasts are at liberty to disagree!). However, Mexico and the United States are not one large tangle of opuntias; hiding underneath rocks and large agaves are many small, globular plants. Hiding is the appropriate word; Mexico is not carpeted with mammillarias, the small cacti have to be sought out. It takes a skilled and experienced eye to spot these cacti in the dry season when they have shrunk back into the earth and are covered with dust.

Ancistrocactus

These are by no means the easiest of the North American cacti to cultivate. They have large fleshy roots and need to be grown in a very open compost if they are not to lose these roots. Ours promptly lost its roots, but has been perfectly happy grafted. Many plants offered for sale are imported, and these are very beautifully spined. *Ancistrocactus* come from Texas and Mexico; they are globular plants with hooked central spines, and the small flowers are carried on top.

A. scheeri is the species most frequently seen in cultivation. This is a solitary, slow-growing plant with strong spines, yellowish in colour. The funnel-shaped flowers are yellowish-green, and about 2·5 cm. (1 in.) long.

Cacti of North America

Astrophytum

Astrophytum have been known to cultivation for about 140 years, and are ideal plants for anyone with limited space who wishes to specialise in a genus. There are only four species, and a small number of varieties, all of which are attractive. They are Mexican plants and need as much sun as possible; they should also be grown in a porous soil.

Astrophytums hybridise amongst themselves quite freely. We have a plant which is a cross between *A. asterias* and *A. capricorne*; it has more vigour than either of its parent species, and is never out of flower during the summer. Whilst we are not suggesting the indiscriminate crossing of astrophytum species, if a hybrid should come your way, it is well worth giving it bench space.

A. asterias looks rather like a sea-urchin. It is a flattened hemisphere, with about 8 spineless ribs; the greyish-green epidermis is covered with white spots. These vary from specimen to specimen, some plants are almost plain green, whilst there are occasionally exceptionally beautiful ones densely covered with silvery spots. Most cultivated plants reach a diameter of about 10 cm. (4 in.); however, Viereck published an account of the plants he has seen in their habitat, and he records specimens up to 22 cm. (9 in.) across.

Our experience with imported specimens has not been encouraging. They died. Seed is easily available, and fresh astrophytum seed germinates quickly. Seedlings left on their own roots have had a high infant mortality rate, but grafted, they have grown vigorously and flowered freely when less than 2·5 cm. (1 in.) across. The pale yellow flowers were larger than the plant. The base of the petals is orange-red.

A. capricorne. We have never found this an easy plant to grow; it loses its roots at the slightest sign of overwatering. However, it flowers when a very small specimen. In appearance *A. capricorne* is cylindrical, eventually reaching a height of about 30 cm. (1 ft.). It has about 9 ribs, with long, intertwining spines. The epidermis is of a greyish-green colour, and covered with white spots. The plant flowers as a seedling; the flowers are pale yellow with an orange-red blotch at the base of the petals.

Cacti of North America

There are several varieties of *A. capricorne*, the commonest is *A. capricorne* var. *senile*. This is a larger plant than the preceding with few white markings and very long spines.

A. capricorne var. *aureum* is similar to the above variety but has more white scales and the young spines are yellow.

A. capricorne var. *major* is also listed as *A. capricorne* var. *crassispinum*. This is a large form of *A. capricorne*; the flowers are said to lack the red throat.

A. capricorne var. *minus* makes a height of only about 10 cm. (4 in.), and the flowers are also small.

A. capricorne var. *niveum* is perhaps the most beautiful variety. It is a large plant, completely covered with white scales.

A. myriostigma is probably the easiest member of this genus to cultivate; it grows well and flowers readily. With age it becomes a cylindrical plant about 20 cm. (8 in.) in diameter. The dark green skin is so completely covered with silvery scales that the plant appears to be carved out of greyish rock. This species is spineless but has very prominent areoles, which gives the plant the appearance of having been buttoned into its skin. The number of ribs has been known to range from 3 to 8. The usual number is 5. Specimens with 4 ribs are known as var. *quadricostata*. Some 4-sided seedlings have a nasty habit of suddenly throwing a 5th rib, proving that they do not belong to a 'variety'. We have a plant about 7 cm. (2¾ in.) across which has remained 4-ribbed so far. It produces large numbers of small, sweetly scented flowers. One year, for no apparent reason, it set seed, although no other astrophytum was in flower at the time. The seed was fertile, the seedlings variable. The majority had 5 ribs and the 4-ribbed ones are still too young to be certain of them staying that way. The flowers of *A. myriostigma* are yellow with a reddish throat; those of var. *quadricostata* are clear yellow and smaller.

Astrophytum myriostigma has several other varieties described by nurserymen, although many botanists consider them to be only 'forms'.

Var. *coahuilensis* is even more densely covered with scales than the species. It reaches a height of 60 cm. (2 ft.).

Var. *columnare* in its native desert makes a column about 2 m. (6 ft.) high.

Var. *nudum* is, as the name implies, quite naked; a dark green plant without a single scale. It has 5 ribs. Before the last war, Herr R. Gräser set out to produce a 4-sided *nudum*. He crossed a *quadricostata* with a *nudum*. The first generation of plants (the F_1) had about half the number of scales of the *quadricostata*, and the 5-ribbed plants outnumbered the 4-ribbed. By crossing the F_1 generation amongst themselves, he obtained all possible combinations of characteristics, including a few 4-sided *nudum*. His aim was to 'fix' this character. Doubtless this astrophytum fell a victim to the war, as we have never seen it advertised.

Var. *potosina* has fewer scales than the ordinary species. The small flowers are clear yellow. The variety *tulensis* may have as many as 10 ribs, although 5 is usual. The ribs are very acute and the large, yellow flowers have a red base.

A. ornatum does not bloom until it is a large plant and is one of the least likely of this genus to flower in cultivation. The only specimen we have seen in bloom was over 15 cm. (6 in.) high. In its native habitat, *A. ornatum* will reach a height of about 1 m. (39 in.) and a diameter of almost 30 cm. (1 ft.). The plant has 8 ribs and stout amber coloured spines. The stem is covered with bands of silvery scales, and the large flowers are yellow. This astrophytum is thought to be a hybrid between *A. myriostigma* and an echinocactus. There are at least two varieties, *mirbellii* with honey yellow spines, and the body completely covered with scales, and *glabrescens*, which has very few scales.

Bergerocactus

Bergerocactus is a monotypic genus, the single species, *B. emoryi* is found in southern California and Baja California. With the clearing of land, it is becoming scarce on the mainland, but is still found on the islands off the coast of California. It is a clustering cactus, the old stems dying off after reaching their full length of about 60 cm. (2 ft.). They are less than 5 cm. (2 in.) across and have many ribs (about 16), covered with needle-like yellow spines. The bright yellow flowers are about 5 cm. (2 in.) long, carried on the ends of the stems.

One odd thing about this cactus is the dispersal of the seeds. As the fruit ripens, the remains of the dead flower are forced to one side by the pressure within the seed-pod. The red pulp, with the seeds embedded in it, is then slowly extruded like tooth paste through the small pore at the apex of the fruit. Apparently ber-gerocactus is the only member of the *Cactaceae* to disperse its seed in this manner. In cultivation, these plants need a bright, sunny position and not too low a winter temperature.

Coloradoa

C. mesa-verde is a small, globular plant, not often seen in collec-tions. It has many radial spines and hooked centrals. The tubercles are rather like those of a mammillaria. It comes from Colorado, and New Mexico.

Coryphantha

The *Coryphantha* are found growing in the south-western United States and Mexico. They are small, globular, or some-times cylindrical cacti, divided into tubercles. The large flowers are carried near the top of the plant. Coryphanthas do not grow quite so quickly from seed as the closely related mammillarias, nor are they as easy to flower. But they have attractive spine forma-tions, and are always good to look at. The species native to grass-lands are easy to grow, whilst those from the extreme desert regions are more prone to succumb to damp conditions and need a very porous soil.

C. bumamma is sometimes considered a variety of *C. elephantidens* and is one of the easier species to cultivate. It is a dark green globular plant with strong spines and yellow flowers.

C. clava is another good species to cultivate. It is cylindrical with yellow spines. The yellow flowers are up to 8 cm. (3 in.) across.

C. cornifera is one of the extreme desert species. It is a globular plant about 12 cm. (4¾ in.) high with yellow radial spines and a very stout, brown, central spine. The flowers are yellow.

C. echinus is another of the desert species. It is also globular and covered with fine white radial spines; each areole may have up to 30 of these, with 3 or 4 long brown centrals. The flowers are yellow.

C. elephantidens is often seen in cultivation. It is a globular plant up to 14 cm. (5½ in.) high with 6 to 8 strong, brownish, radial spines and no centrals. The pink flowers may be as large as 10 cm. (4 in.).

C. pallida is one of the easier species. Again globular and about 12 cm. (4¾ in.) across, it has about 20 white radial spines and 3 centrals. The flowers are yellow.

C. sulcata is more difficult; it is a clustering greyish-green plant with comb-like white radials and also with yellow flowers.

C. vivipara is frequently seen in collections. It is a freely-clustering greyish plant with numerous white radials and reddish flowers. It is almost hardy.

Cumarinia

C. odorata, once *Neolloydia odorata*, is a small, clustering, globular plant, with cylindrical tubercles and hooked spines.

Dolichothele

Dolichothele are closely related to mammillarias, but the tubercles are much more pronounced. The flowers also are larger than those of the mammillarias, and instead of circlets of small flowers, dolichotheles produce 1 or 2 large bright yellow ones. These cacti have very thick tap roots and the spherical body is bright green in colour with rather weak spines. Young plants are solitary, but slowly form off-sets with age. We have found dolichotheles very easy to grow and flower. There are at least 6 species, and they are found in southern Texas and northern and central Mexico.

D. baumii, with its small tubercles, resembles a mammillaria, in fact Borg classes it as such. It is a clustering plant with heads about 6 cm. (2¼ in.) across, and up to 35 slender white radial spines. The central spines are stouter and 5 or 6 in number. It has the typical large yellow flowers of this genus, about 2–3 cm. (1 in.) long, funnel-shaped.

D. longimamma is in our opinion the best of the dolichotheles. It has very long tubercles, which in the variety *gigantothele* may reach a length of 7 cm. (2¾ in.). There are 5–7 white radial spines and 1–3 centrals. The flowers are 6 cm. (2¼ in.) across.

D. melaleuca is a small species with brown spines. We have found it difficult to flower.

D. sphaerica is a small plant with reddish central spines. The flowers are about 6 cm. (2¼ in.) across and funnel-shaped.

D. surculosa is a small clustering plant with heads about 3 cm. (1¼ in.) across. There are about 15 white radial spines and one brownish central.

D. uberiformis is considered by some botanists to be a variety of *D. longimamma*. It has stouter tubercles than the latter, and no central spines. The flowers are also smaller.

Echinocereus

The *Echinocereus* are found in the south-western United States and Mexico. We have grown a number of species; they are hardy plants with magnificent flowers. Our echinocerei are kept dry all winter, and on occasion they have been below freezing without ill effects. We find that the vigorous prostrate species are more difficult to flower than the slower-growing erect ones. These latter need to be grown in a particularly porous soil; if allowed to become at all waterlogged they will lose their roots. Seed of echinocerei is easily available, and we find that they are easy to raise.

Buxbaum divided *Echinocereus* into three groups, depending on their habit of growth. From a grower's point of view, this grouping by appearance is very convenient and we shall use it here.

1. Plants with weak spines   Series *Subinermis*
2. Prostrate, mat-forming plants   ,,   *Prostrati*
3. Erect plants, branching from base   ,,   *Erecti*
      (a) Many ribs, close areoles   Subseries *Longiseti*
      (b) Many ribs, pectinate radials   ,,   *Pectinati*
      (c) Less erect, forming large mats   ,,   *Decalophi*

The naming of echinocerei is difficult since there is a great variability amongst these plants. In New Mexico Taylor Marshall found a plant of the *Echinocereus dasyacanthus* type with a purple flower on one side of the plant and a yellow one on the other. Some so-called 'species' change their characteristics with change of locality, and are merely geographical variants.

Cacti of North America

E. knippelianus was one of the first echinocerei that we owned, and it is still flowering for us many years later. It is a dark green, 5-ribbed plant, about 5 cm. (2 in.) across. Our specimen is slow-growing and has remained solitary. The spines are very weak and the pale pink flowers are small for this genus, but are produced in quantity.

E. pulchellus is a branching plant; the greyish-green stems are about 5 cm. (2 in.) thick, and have 11–13 ribs with short spines. The small flowers are pink.

E. subinermis is another branching plant. The stems are 8–9 cm. (about 3½ in.) thick, and have 5–8 ribs, with very short spines. The yellow flowers are larger than those of the above two plants.

PROSTRATI GROUP

Most of these plants are best grown in wide pans so that they can sprawl outwards. They eventually make large specimens.

E. blanckii has sprawling stems about 35 cm. (14 in.) long and 3 cm. (1¼ in.) thick. The radial spines are white, and the large flowers are violet.

E. pentalophus has mostly sprawling stems, up to about 12 cm. (5 in.) long. The spines are yellowish, and the reddish-purple flowers are about 8 cm. (3 in.) across. In our experience this is one of the easier echinocerei to flower.

E. procumbens has prostrate stems about 15 cm. (6 in.) long with whitish spines. The flowers are violet.

E. salm-dyckianus is a much-branched plant with stems about 20 cm. (8 in.) long, armed with yellow spines. The flowers are red.

E. scheeri is a semi-prostrate plant with stems up to 22 cm. (8–9 in.) long. The radial spines are yellow and the centrals brown. The pink flowers are about 12 cm. (4¾ in.) long.

ERECTI GROUP

(a) *Longiseti*

There is only one species in this group, *E. delaetii*. This has very long white hairs, rather like *Cephalocereus senilis*. It is found in Mexico at altitudes of 2,200 m. (7,000 ft.) and needs plenty of sunshine, combined with a cold winter rest. The pale pink flowers are about 6 cm. (2¼ in.) across, but are rarely produced in cultivation; probably the light intensity is insufficient in northern areas.

(b) *Pectinati*

The *Pectinati* group of *Echinocereus* are not the easiest to grow, needing a very porous soil, but flower freely as quite small plants. With their upright habit and slow growth, old specimens can easily be housed in 10-cm. (4-in.) pots. Many pectinate echino-cerei have been given specific rank; the American botanist, Taylor Marshall, has suggested that they are all really forms of *E. dasyacanthus*.

E. baileyi is found in Oklahoma and is a columnar plant which can reach a height of 25 cm. (10 in.). It is covered with rusty-red spines. The large flowers are a deep magenta.

E. dasyacanthus. The stems of this cactus are about 7 cm. (2¾ in.) across and 23 cm. (9 in.) high. The greyish plant body is completely covered with reddish-brown spines. The flowers are canary-yellow, but this species is not as free-flowering as other members of the group.

E. oklahomensis, true to its name, is found in south-west Oklahoma. The stems may reach a length of 16 cm. (6¼ in.), and have 13–15 ribs. The spines are a rust colour. The magenta flowers are about 10 cm. (4 in.) across.

E. pectinatus is one of the most easily obtained in this subgroup. The thick stems branch from the base and are completely covered with the comb-like white radial spines, from which the plant gets its name. The young growth has pinkish spines. The pink flowers are about 8 cm. (3 in.) long. A number of varieties exist of *E. pectinatus*—perhaps the best known is *reichenbachii*, which has many popular names, including 'Lace Cactus' and 'Strawberry Cactus' (the fruits are edible). *Reichenbachii* is the most northerly and hardiest of the varieties of *E. pectinatus*. The flowers are large and magenta-coloured.

Another variety is *E. pectinatus rigidissimus*; this is the Arizona 'Rainbow Cactus'. The spine colour varies from white to pink or brown during the year, so that the plant has zones of different coloured spines, giving rise to its common name. The pink flowers are about 7 cm. (2¾ in.) long.

E. viridiflorus is well named, having usually greenish flowers about 2.5 cm. (1 in.) long. It is a freely branching plant with spines of variable colour; they may be white or brown and are arranged in zones.

(c) *Decalophi*

This includes a number of well-known plants, but they do not flower as freely as the above.

E. engelmannii is a freely branching plant with stems about 25 cm. (10 in.) high, covered with long stiff spines. The centrals are white and the radials yellow. The purplish flower is about 8 cm. (3 in.) long.

E. fendleri has stems about 15 cm. (6 in.) long with yellow or brownish spines. The purplish flowers are about 8 cm. (3 in.) long.

E. stramineus has erect branching stems up to 25 cm. (10 in.) high, covered with long straw-coloured spines. The purple flowers may be up to 12 cm. (4¾ in.) long.

Echinofossulocactus

These cacti are still frequently listed under the much shorter name, *Stenocactus*, but *Echinofossulocactus* is the correct generic name according to the Nomenclature Code. No doubt many amateur collectors prefer to keep to the former name, if only to avoid laborious label writing, but in doing so they infringe the botanic Law of Priority!

These plants are native to Mexico, where they are found in sun-baked mountainous regions. They are small cacti about 15 cm. high by 12 cm. wide (6 in. by 4¾ in.) and rarely cluster. It is very easy for even a novice grower to recognise an echinofossulocactus since they have characteristic wavy ribs. The usual number of ribs is 30 or 40, but *E. multicostatus* has at least 100, and *E. coptonogonus* fewer. The spines are quite spectacular; although not many in number, they are long and broad. The small flowers are produced by the new areoles on top of the plant. Their colours are rather dull, pink, white or yellowish.

98

The actual number of species is in dispute, and is probably very few, although some authors describe as many as 22 to 30. One reason for this confusion is that echinofossulocacti hybridise easily, even in the native state. Some of the plants we have as species may well be natural hybrids.

These cacti are easy to cultivate, needing a porous soil and plenty of water in summer, with as much sun as our climate permits, and in winter, a cool, dry rest. Many species flower as small plants.

E. albatus has yellowish-white spines, consisting of about 10 bristle-like radials and 4 larger centrals. The upper central is a flattened spine about 4·5 cm. ($1\frac{3}{4}$ in.) long. The flowers are white.

E. coptonogonus has only 10–14 ribs, which should easily distinguish it from the rest of the genus. There are 3–5 spines, up to 3·5 cm. ($1\frac{1}{2}$ in.) long. When new, they are red, but fade to a greyish colour with age. The flowers are whitish.

E. hastatus. The name means 'spear-like', and this is meant to describe the spines. The 5 or 6 radials are up to 3 cm. ($1\frac{1}{4}$ in.) long, and the central is flat and about 4 cm. ($1\frac{1}{2}$ in.) long. Both the spines and the flowers are yellowish.

E. lamellosus has about 35 ribs and white spines, tipped brown. The radials are 2 cm. ($\frac{3}{4}$ in.) long, and the one central is flattened and around 4 cm. ($1\frac{1}{2}$ in.) long. The flowers are pinkish.

E. lancifer has spines like lances in the eyes of the botanist who named it. They are white and the large flowers are pink.

E. lloydii has white, needle-like radials and 3 brown central curving spines, the upper one being papery. The flowers are pink.

E. multicostatus is noted for the number of its ribs and its variable spine length. The yellowish spines may be anything from 5 mm. to 8 cm. long ($\frac{1}{4}$ to 3 in.). The flowers are large and white.

E. phyllacanthus received its name because its spines are flattened and leaf-like. They may reach a length of 8 cm. (3 in.) and are red in colour, fading to brown with age. The flowers are yellowish.

Echinomastus

These are small, usually solitary cacti with many ribs and short spines. The ribs are notched into warts and the areoles woolly. Cultivation is not difficult and flowers are freely produced. The

Cacti of North America

natural habitat is Mexico, Texas and Arizona. The Zürich catalogue decribes 11 species. *E. macdowellii* is the species most often found in collections and is one of the most beautiful. The solitary pale green stem is about 10 cm. (4 in.) high and 6 cm. (2¼ in.) diameter. There are about 20 ribs, and the areoles bear white wool. The 15–20 white spines are up to 2 cm. (¾ in.) long and the 3–4 straw-coloured centrals about twice this length. The bright pink flowers are about 5 cm. (2 in.) long.

Escobaria

Escobaria are small, clustering cacti, nicely spined, and they flower as young plants. The pale flowers are produced on the young areoles near the top of the plant, and are followed by bright red berries, more eye-catching than the flowers. They are most attractive plants. However, the ideal plant does not seem to exist. The drawback with escobarias is that they rot very easily if overwatered. They need a very porous soil, and even with that, cautious watering.

At one time, escobarias were included in the genus *Mammillaria*. There are about 11 species, occurring mainly in Mexico, New Mexico and Texas.

E. chaffeyi is a white-spined plant which produces its pale pinkish flowers when very small. It is slow-growing.

E. tuberculosa is the species most frequently seen. This is a clustering plant with cylindrical stems. It has 20–30 short, slender radial spines which are white; the centrals are darker. The flowers are about 2·5 cm. (1 in.) across, and violet-pink in colour. This species has a number of varieties; these differ mainly in the colour and number of spines.

Glandulicactus   Now included under *Neolloydia*

Gymnocactus   Now included under *Neolloydia*

Hamatocactus

Hamatocactus are small cacti which do well in cultivation; there cannot be many collections which have not included *Hamato-*

cactus setispinus at some time. There are 3 species described. They occur in Mexico and Texas.

H. hamatacanthus is a cylindrical plant, old specimens may reach a height of 60 cm. (2 ft.). The young spines are deep red in colour but turn whitish with age. The radials can reach a length of 7 cm. (2¾ in.) and the centrals 12 cm. (4¾ in.). But these measurements were presumably made on imported plants, and seedlings grown in this country are unlikely to be so heavily armed. The flowers are large and yellow, with a red throat. *H. hamatacanthus* is certainly a giant among the hamatocacti. Buxbaum includes this plant with the ferocacti. There are 4 varieties, differing in the size and number of their spines, *crassispina*, *gracilispina*, *brevispina* and *sinuata*.

H. setispinus is a very free-flowering plant, specimens only 2·5 cm. (1 in.) across producing their yellow, red-throated blooms. As an adult it is a globular plant, about 12 cm. (4¾ in.) across, with white spines which can reach a length of 4 cm. (1½ in.). There are 4 varieties, *cachetianus*, *hamatus*, *mierensis*, and *orcuttii*.

H. uncinatus is a cylindrical plant, ultimately reaching a height of about 20 cm. (8 in.). It has long, hooked radial spines, which are red, fading to white with age. With imported plants the centrals may be 12 cm. (4¾ in.) long. The flowers are smaller than those of the preceding species, and of a reddish-brown colour. There is a variety, *wrightii,* with longer, redder spines.

Mammillaria

Some collectors consider the *Mammillaria* to be *the* genus. There is a specialist society catering solely for the mammillaria enthusiast. Certainly there are enough species to fill a greenhouse the size of an aircraft hangar, and although there is not a great deal of variety in their flowers, there is an enormous difference in the spines and habit of growth of the various species. Some plants form clusters literally the size of cushions, whilst other species can be housed in an 8-cm. (3-in.) flower pot. There are mammillarias for all growers; easy, fast-growing species for the beginner, plants that are so touchy that even the experts have difficulty in keeping them alive, and in between these two extremes, hundreds of species for the rest of us to fill our greenhouses.

The great centre of the mammillaria population is Mexico. From here they spread north into the United States (Arizona, California, New Mexico, and Texas), and south into Honduras, Guatemala, Columbia, and Venezuela. They are also found on some of the islands of the West Indies and off the coast of Baja California. However, if somebody shows you a mammillaria and you give Mexico as its homeland, you will seldom be wrong. In passing, it may be noted that the species from the extreme deserts of Baja California are often difficult in cultivation. Mammillarias are found in widely differing places; some grow on sandy areas along the shores, whilst others are found in barren mountain regions. The range of some species is very limited; one or two will be found in a particular locality, then there will be no more plants for miles, when probably another species will crop up.

In appearance mammillarias are low-growing plants, which frequently cluster. Their most notable characteristic is the absence of ribs and the presence of tubercles (the name is derived from the Latin *mammilla*, meaning nipples or teats). The spines are carried on the tips of these protuberances, and are very variable in the different species. Some spines are short and stiff, some long and curved, whilst others are hair- or feather-like. The small, bell-shaped flowers are borne in circlets around the top of the plant. They are formed on the previous year's growth, so that if a plant has not grown well one year it is unlikely to flower well the next. The flowers are most commonly cream or pale yellow in colour, or a magenta-red. One can generalise with some truth and say that the former will flower when young, but the red-flowered species need to be larger plants before doing so. One notable exception is *Mammillaria zeilmanniana* which produces rings of bright magenta flowers on plants as small as 2·5 cm. (1 in.) across. The flowers of many species are followed by long, brightly coloured seed-pods, which frequently decorate the plant for months, often remaining until the following year's flowers appear, so that the ring of flowers has another of bright red pods beneath it.

Most mammillarias can be easily propagated. Seed is freely available, and usually the young plants grow well; if the correct species are chosen they will reach flowering size when two or three years old. Clustering species can be broken up and the heads rooted; this will give a flowering size specimen quickly. Some growers have produced fresh plants by rooting tubercles. We have never tried this ourselves, but since some of our plants with prominent tubercles have grown new heads at the tips of the tubercles, it seems likely that if the tubercles had been removed, we would have had new plants.

The genus *Mammillaria* is very large; 300 species have been accepted, and many new ones are still being discovered by botanical explorers. There have been a number of attempts to split up this rather unwieldy genus. However, many of these segregate genera do not seem to have much popular support, and we shall follow the example of the seed catalogues, calling them *Mamillaria*, except for those generally accepted as separate.

For those who may be interested, Dr Alwin Berger, in his work *Kakteen*, divided the genus into two sections, *Hydrochylus* (the species with watery sap) and *Galactochylus* (species with milky sap). These two sections were subdivided into 10 others. One objection to this classification is that there are species having milky sap at one time of the year, but if you stick a needle into them later on, you will find that their sap has changed; it is clear and watery. This scheme is set out in Borg's *Cacti*. Buxbaum has devised yet another and more complicated scheme, which can be found in his book *Cactus Culture based on Biology*. But, briefly, if you meet plants with names like *Mammilloydia, Leptocladodia, Chilita, Bartochella* and *Pseudomammillaria,* they are, or were, in the collective genus *Mammillaria,* depending on whether or not taxonomists accept Buxbaum's views.

In the following list of mammillarias, we have tried to give a range of plants, including easy species which will flourish on a window-sill, and also some of the rarities which may offer a challenge to the experienced grower. We like to think that they all have one thing in common; they are attractive additions to one's collection.

M. aureilanata is a slow-growing, solitary species, with a thickened storage root. The plant grows in rock fissures in the mountainous regions of Mexico, the tap-root giving a firm anchorage, and also storing water against a dry period. The stem is covered with numerous fine radial spines of a beautiful yellow colour. This is a spring-flowering species, the large white, or pale pink flowers opening in March. There is a variety, *alba*, in which the radial spines are white and the flowers pink.

M. blossfeldiana is one of the slow-growing species that is not often seen. It is a native of the coastal regions of Baja California. The plant has a thickened storage root and a globular body that rarely clusters. The hooked central spines are black tipped and show up well against the yellowish-white radials. The large flowers are white with a red stripe down the centre of each petal. Many of the large flowered mammillarias, with hooked spines, are difficult to keep for any length of time. The young seedlings are sometimes difficult; those that survive flower beautifully for three or four years, and then inexplicably die. We have had an imported specimen of *M. blossfeldiana* for about a year now, so it is too early to say if it is going the way of many hooked-spined mammillarias, but if you have a species which fades away after five or six years, it may well be the nature of the plant rather than your faulty cultivation.

M. bocasana must be one of the most popular cacti in cultivation. It is easily raised from seed, and rapidly clusters to form large 'cushions'. When too large, these clumps may be broken up and the pieces re-rooted. The bluish-green plant body is covered with a network of silky white radial spines. The centrals are hooked; this is one hooked-spined species which is easy to grow, but the creamy flowers are small. However, they appear in large numbers during the late spring. We have seen specimens of *M. bocasana* with beautiful satiny-pink flowers; they were said to be hybrids with *M. erythrosperma*. This seems to be a case of an offspring inheriting the best points of both parents.

M. bombycina is a cylindrical plant and clusters from the lower stem with age. The areoles have 30–40 white radial spines and 4 reddish centrals. Although this plant has as many spines as *M. bocasana*, they do not give the 'halo' effect of the latter. The small red flowers open around May, but they are not produced on small plants.

M. boolii is one of the larger-flowered mammillarias, the pinkish-lavender flowers reaching a diameter of 5 cm. (2 in.). This species has a tap-root which anchors it into the soil on the windy hills of

Mexico. The tubercles carry 20 white radial spines and a brown tipped central. This is one of the solitary mammillarias, but it can be raised from seed without great difficulty.

M. brauneana is usually unbranched. It is globular when young, becoming more elongated with age. The numerous white bristly spines give the plant a sparkling appearance. The flowers are purplish in colour, but this is not one of the most free-flowering of mammillarias.

M. camptotricha, the Bird's-nest Cactus, has insignificant whitish flowers, but they make up for their lack of size with their sweet, lime tree-flower perfume. The plant clusters freely and has a rather straggly appearance, due to the long slender tubercles and the interlacing twisted spines.

M. candida is surely one of the most beautiful mammillarias in cultivation. Unfortunately, it is not one of the easiest, being very prone to rot at the neck. In its native Mexico this cactus grows amongst chalk scree where its roots extend for about 60 cm. (2 ft.). The plant is spherical and is closely covered with short white spines. The flowers appear in the early summer and are white with a pink stripe. *M. candida* var. *rosea* is even more beautiful than its species. The central spines on the young growth are a rose-pink colour.

M. celsiana is a single-headed plant when young, but mature specimens cluster. There are about 30 white radial spines and the 4–6 centrals are yellow. The spines almost completely cover the plant body. This mammillaria flowers in the late spring; the rather small flowers are carmine. This is not a fast grower, but we have found it easier to keep than *M. candida*.

M. cowperae is a solitary globose plant, from Mexico, reaching a height of about 11 cm. (4¼ in.) and with pronounced tubercles. The sap is watery. The axils contain white hair, the numerous radial spines are thin and white; there are 8 pale yellow centrals, 2 of them hooked. The bell-shaped flowers appear from March to May, are greenish-white in colour and about 2 cm. (¾ in.) wide.

M. deherdtiana is one of the most recently discovered species, having been found in May 1969 in the state of Oaxaca, Mexico. It is a small, solitary plant with watery sap, and tubercles up to 1 cm. (⅜ in.) long. The radial spines are numerous (30–60), short and spreading, the upper curved. They are yellow or glistening white. The few centrals are reddish-brown in colour. The funnel-shaped flower is up to 5 cm. (2 in.) across with flesh-coloured outer petals and rose-violet inner ones.

M. elegans is a globular plant when young, but elongates with age and eventually clusters. It is closely spined, with about 30 white radials; the centrals are also white, with brown tips. The small purplish-red flowers open in April.

M. elongata consists, as the name suggests, of long, finger-shaped shoots; they are freely clustering. It is an easy species to grow and flower, the creamy flowers appearing in March or April. There are about 20 radial spines which give the areoles a rather star-like appearance. There is considerable variation in spine colour; white, yellow, brown, and even deep red.

M. erythrosperma is a plant frequently seen in collections. It soon forms a large 'cushion'. Despite its popularity, we have not found it an easy cactus to grow. Water collects between the numerous heads, and if you are not very careful with the watering, your beautiful plant becomes a soggy mess. There are around 20 white radials, and 1–3 brown centrals. The flowers are a satiny pink and are followed by vivid red berries.

M. fasciculata is a species that is not only found in Mexico but also in Arizona. It forms large clumps, often on the banks of dried-up rivers, where it gets some shade from larger cacti and rocks. But because it thrives in shade from the Mexican sun, it does not necessarily mean that it needs shading from the paler British version. Like many other hooked-spined mammillarias, *M. fasciculata* needs particularly good drainage, and is not easy to raise from seed. The columnar heads have white radial spines and hooked black centrals. The flowers are white with a pink mid stripe, and appear in late summer to autumn.

M. glassii is one of the newer species from Nuevo Leon, Mexico. It is a caespitose plant, sprouting from near the base and with watery sap. The heads are globose, from 3–10 cm. ($1\frac{1}{4}$–4 in.) across, old specimens only reaching the larger size. The appearance is silky, due to the white bristles in the axils, and the numerous hair-like, white radial spines. The centrals are golden-amber, about 8 in number, 1 hooked. The pink to green flowers appear in March and April, and remain open for several days, but only opening completely in full sun. They are small and tube-like. *M. goldii* was discovered in 1968 and is closely related to *M. saboae* (q.v.). It is solitary or sparingly caespitose, about 2·5 cm. (1 in.) in diameter. The pinkish-brown flowers are up to 3 cm. (1¼ in.) across. It comes from Sonora, Mexico.

M. gracilis is found in many collections; the clusters fall apart so easily that it sometimes becomes a problem to find good homes for all the shoots. It is often sold under the name *M. fragilis*. The cylindrical stems are pale green in colour, and covered with star-like radial spines. The creamy flowers open around April.

M. guelzowiana is one of those hooked-spined mammillarias with magnificent flowers, which are so difficult to raise from seed and which never seem to last long in cultivation. The globular stems branch from the base and are covered with numerous white radial spines; up to 80 may be present. The single central is hooked. Out of flower, this species rather resembles *M. bocasana*. The flowers are a deep purple-red on a long tube, and are 2·5 cm. (1 in.) across.

M. guiengolensis is a fairly recent discovery, being described in 1962. It was found in Oaxaca, Mexico. It is caespitose, forming clumps, the individual heads being up to 10 cm. (4 in.) high and 4 cm. (1½ in.) diameter, a pale green in colour, with watery sap. The radial spines are pale yellow and glassy, 7 mm. (¼ in.) long. The centrals are slightly longer, darker and hooked.

M. hahniana is a variable species. We have seen neat specimens with short hair and others with hair so long that it would have done credit to *Cephalocereus senilis*. As a young plant it is solitary, but clusters with age; in its native habitat old specimens form large clumps. The greyish-green stem has up to 30 fine white, radial spines to each areole. These are short and interlacing. The long hair is formed by the bristles growing from the axils between the tubercles, which in some plants reach a length of 5 cm. (2 in.). The small reddish-purple flowers open in midsummer.

M. herrerae is a beautiful miniature mammillaria, but like many of the tight, white-spined species, it is very prone to rot off. We wish we had tried grafting our specimen! Unfortunately, *M. herrerae* is not often offered for sale, so we have not had a second chance at growing it. This is a globular species, about 3·5 cm. (1½ in.) across and is densely covered with white spines.

The 100-odd radials are arranged in a star-like formation. The large rose-pink flowers open in April.

M. klissingiana is a very handsome species with close white spines, which remain white all the way down the column. This is a slow-growing, cylindrical species, about 10 cm. (4 in.) across, which forms some branches with age. There are 30–35 white radials and 2–4 white centrals, tipped brown. Our own specimen is about 23 cm. (9 in.) high and is only just beginning to branch; it has not flowered. The rose-coloured flowers are said to open in the late spring.

M. lanata is a slow-growing plant with tight white spines, rather similar to the above. The stem is short-cylindrical; it is said to cluster from the base. Our specimen, which is about 10 years old, has neither clustered nor flowered. The flowers should be pale pink in colour and produced in the spring. There are about 12–20 white radials.

M. lindsayi from south-west Chihuahua, Mexico, growing in partial shade on the walls of canyons, is a clustering plant, forming large clumps. The individual heads are globular, up to 15 cm. (6 in.) across. The sap is milky. The axils contain dense white wool, and long white bristles, nearly covering the tubercles. There are 10–14 radial spines and 2–4 centrals, about 1 cm. ($\frac{3}{8}$ in.) long and reddish-yellow in colour.

M. longiflora is one of the largest-flowered mammillarias, and is also one of the most difficult to keep. It is another of those hooked-spined species which seem to be short-lived. It is a shortly-cylindrical plant, which clusters from the base when young. There are 25–30 straw-coloured radial spines and 4 brown centrals; the lowest are hooked. The pink flowers appear in May; they are about 2·5 cm. (1 in.) long and about the same width. Very young specimens of this plant, seedlings about 2·5 cm. across, will often produce flowers almost as large as themselves.

M. louisae is occasionally branched, up to about 3 cm. ($1\frac{1}{4}$ in.) high. It is found near the beach on the coast of Baja California, Mexico. There are about 11 radial spines, needle-like, 5–7 mm. ($\frac{1}{4}$–$\frac{3}{8}$ in.) long, light brown in colour, with darker tips. The 4 centrals are slightly longer, the lowest one hooked. The flowers are up to 4 cm. ($1\frac{1}{2}$ in.) wide, brownish-green outside and pink inside.

M. mainae has a wide distribution, from Arizona to northern Mexico. The stems are about 10 cm. (4 in.) high, and around 5 cm. (2 in.) across; old plants cluster from the base. The spines are yellowish, 10–15 radials with 1 or 2 long hooked centrals. The flowers occur in the late spring and are large, up to 2·5 cm. (1 in.) in diameter. The petals are pale pink with a deeper pink mid-stripe. This mammillaria can take a lot of water in its growing period.

M. microcarpa is another of the hooked-spined species with large flowers, about 4 cm. (1½ in.) across, which are difficult to raise from seed, and rather short-lived. But many growers consider the trouble well worth while because of the pink, scented flowers. This species covers a very large area, California, Texas, through the southern United States into Mexico. With such an extended habitat, it is not surprising that there is considerable variation in form. The plant body may be either globular or cylindrical and branches freely. There are 20–30 radials which vary in colour from white through yellow to buff. The hooked central spine is light brown to black. The fruit of this cactus exists in two forms, red berries, or small green fruits formed from the later flowers.

M. microhelia is a popular species. The stem is solitary or sprouting, reaching a height of about 15 cm. (6 in.) and 4 cm. (1½ in.) thick. The radial spines are numerous and widely spreading, golden-yellow in colour. The longer centrals are reddish-brown. The flowers are pale greenish-yellow, or sometimes pink.

M. morricalii is another new species from Chihuahua. The stem is usually simple, sometimes forming small clumps of 2–5 heads of a yellowish appearance. The individual heads are oval or short cylindrical, about 5–10 cm. (2–4 in.) tall. The sap is watery. The radial spines are about 20 in number, fine, stiff and pale yellow. There is one stiff, hooked central, orange with a dark tip. The flowers are about 2 cm. (¾ in.) in diameter, of a pink to orange colour.

M. parkinsonii has stems about 15 cm. (6 in.) high and 8 cm. (3 in.) in diameter; these branch dichotomously to form large clumps. The stems are covered with brilliant white spines, 20–30 radials and usually 2 centrals, the lower one being about 3·5 cm. (1¼ in.) long. The pinkish flowers open in the late summer.

M. pennispinosa is one of the mammillarias that can be recognised at a glance; the feathery brown spines are unique. There are 16–20 radials and 1 hooked central. This species is found growing in fissures in vertical cliff faces. The plant heads are globular and attached to a thickened tap-root. Some accounts of this mammillaria suggest that only old plants cluster, but this is not our experience. We find that it starts to branch when young, and we now have a 15-cm. (6-in.) pan of it. In many ways it reminds us of *M. plumosa* in its habit of growth. We have not attempted to split the clump and re-root the heads. The creamy-white flowers, with a reddish stripe down the centre of the petals, are formed early in the year, even on young plants.

M. perbella is another of the very clean-looking, white-spined species. It is cylindrical, about 6 cm. (2¼ in.) in diameter, and usually solitary. The spines are white, 14–18 radials and 2 centrals. *M. perbella* flowers in the early summer, the pale pink petals have a darker mid-stripe.

M. plumosa seems to exist in two forms, the more attractive being the one less often seen. One form consists of a cluster of distinct heads, rather like a group of golf balls. The more common form is the shape of a white mound and the separate heads can only be distinguished on careful examination. This is a difficult species to flower; the large greenish-white blooms open in December. Some writers claim that this is a winter-growing plant. We tried carefully watering our specimen all one winter, but the plant did not come into growth until the spring, neither did it flower. The beautiful appearance of this mammillaria is due to the feathery, white radial spines, about 40 to each areole.

M. rhodantha is a very popular plant in cultivation; it is easy to grow and has vividly coloured spines, varying from rich red, through various shades of brown to yellow. Numerous varieties have been created, based on spine colour, although many are probably only environmental variations of the same plant. The stem is cylindrical in shape, about 8 cm. (3 in.) across; mature specimens branch from the base. There are 16–20 radial spines and 4 centrals. The flowers are magenta-red and appear in mid-summer.

M. saboae. This is a new species, noteworthy for being probably the smallest of all the mammillarias, but having some of the largest flowers of any of the genus. The individual heads are only

1–2 cm. ($\frac{3}{8}$–$\frac{3}{4}$ in.) wide and high, although the plant is caespitose. The plant tends to be partially drawn underground. The tubercles are small and the sap watery. The spines are all radials, about 20 in number, short and glassy-white. The funnel-shaped flowers are up to 4 cm. (1$\frac{1}{2}$ in.) wide and long, and of a greenish-pink colour. This mammillaria was found in Chihuahua, at a height of 2,100 m. (7,000 ft.) and exposed to extremes of temperature. This cactus would be a noteworthy addition to any collection, and it is hoped that it will soon become available.

M. schiedeana is one of the prettiest mammillarias in cultivation, and one that is easily recognised. This is a clustering plant; the heads are about 5 cm. (2 in.) across and 10 cm. (4 in.) high. The plant body is dark green and is covered with fine golden radial spines. There are 15 of these to each areole, and no centrals. The creamy flowers are about 1·5 cm. ($\frac{5}{8}$ in.) across and are readily produced in the early summer. This plant needs very careful watering, particularly if grown on its own roots, and the soil must be very porous.

M. sheldonii is another of the large-flowered, hooked-spined mammillarias which are so prone to rot, particularly as young plants. The stem is cylindrical and clusters when the plant is still young; it is greyish-green in colour. There are 10–15 radials and 1–3 centrals, all brown; the lowest central is hooked. The flowers are about 3 cm. (1$\frac{1}{4}$ in.) across and the pale pink petals have a dark pink mid-stripe. They open in the middle of summer, on quite young plants.

M. spinosissima is a variable species. The spines may be white, yellow, various shades of brown, or red. Needless to say, all these spine colours have caused many different names to be given, over 200 of them. However, since changes in environment can alter the spine colour, it is difficult to say how many of these varieties are really distinct. The cylindrical stem is dark green in colour. The areoles have 20–30 radials and 7–15 centrals. The purplish-red flowers are produced in the summer. The variety *sanguinea* is a particularly attractive plant, with red-tipped central spines.

M. theresae is a new species, very similar to *M. saboae*, except that the tubercles are longer and more slender and the flowers violet-pink. It was found on the eastern slopes of the Coneto

Mountains, Durango, Mexico. Both this mammillaria and *M. saboae* appear to have an unusual seed arrangement, as the seeds were found to be retained deep within the body, even on the oldest portions of the plants. It would seem that the seeds rarely germinate in the wild until the parent plant has disintegrated from old age. Germination in cultivation is poor as the seed may need to age for many years before it is viable.

M. wildii is one of the commonest mammillarias in cultivation, which says much for its vigour; clusters 30 cm. (1 ft.) in diameter, with several hundreds of heads, are formed. The stems are about 10 cm. (4 in.) long and 6 cm. (2¼ in.) across. There are 8–10 whitish radials and 3 or 4 yellow central spines, the lower one hooked. The white flowers are produced continuously throughout the summer. There is also a free-flowering cristate form.

M. zeilmanniana is one of the most free-flowering of the mammillarias in our collection; the flowers are a reddish-violet colour and plants less than 2·5 cm. (1 in.) will flower. The stem is cylindrical and forms some branches. There are 15–18 whitish radial spines and 4 brown centrals, the lower one hooked. Occasionally a form of this plant is seen with flowers having a double row of petals.

Neobesseya

There are six or seven species of *Neobesseya* described, but some are very difficult to distinguish as cultivated specimens, and it is possible that they may be varieties or geographical variants of one or two species. The plant most commonly seen in cultivation is *Neobesseya missouriensis*. This is found along the upper reaches of the Missouri river and is especially plentiful in the north-east section of the State of Missouri.

N. missouriensis is a globular plant about 6 cm. (2½ in.) across, which easily forms rooted off-sets. This genus is allied to *Dolichothele*, and the neobesseyas have similar long tubercles. The areoles carry 10–20 fine radial spines, curved and greyish in colour. The pale yellow flowers are borne on top of the plant. This cactus is hardy if kept dry in winter, but rots easily if overwatered at any time. It should be grown in a very open compost.

Neolloydia

The genus *Neolloydia* includes the former genera *Gymnocactus* and *Glandulicactus*. These plants are found in Mexico, and one species is native to Texas. They have an extensive fibrous root system and do well in pans, but they are rather prone to rot at the neck and should be grown in a very porous compost. There are about 5 species described.

N. beguinii is usually solitary in cultivation, and reaches a height of 15 cm. (6 in.). The areoles have 12–20 radial spines, white with dark tips, and one long central. The large violet flowers are carried on the top of the stem, as is characteristic of neolloydias.

N. ceratites has oval greyish stems, up to 10 cm. (4 in.) high. Each areole has 15 greyish spines and 5 or 6 long centrals. The flowers are purple.

N. conoidea also includes *N. texensis,* which is usually considered to be a geographical variant of this species. The cylindrical stems cluster freely; they are greyish-green in colour and about 10 cm. (4 in.) high. There are 16 greyish radials and 4 or 5 black centrals. The flowers are very large for this genus, being about 6 cm. ($2\frac{1}{4}$ in.) broad, and are violet in colour.

N. grandiflora has a similar habit to the above plant. It has 25 white radials and 1 or 2 black centrals. The large flowers are a violet-pink.

N. horripila has a cylindrical stem about 12 cm. ($4\frac{3}{4}$ in.) high, and bluish-green in colour. There are 9 or 10 radials and one central, all white in colour. The deep pinkish-red flowers are about 3 cm. ($1\frac{1}{4}$ in.) long.

Oehmea

Oehmea nelsonii is included as one of the subgenera of *Mammillaria* by Buxbaum; it is often listed as *Dolichothele aylostera* in catalogues. The seeds of this plant are available, we have tried growing them ourselves. They germinated readily, and the seedlings grew rapidly. Then suddenly for no apparent reason, they rotted. Every morning when the seedpans were examined, there was one less plant, until eventually there was none. Not to be discouraged, we tried again the next year, and grafted the seedlings.

By the end of October the last little plant had died. However, the reader should not be disheartened; if he or she has plenty of time and patience, the plants are worth trying to grow from seed, and the attempt may meet with more success.

Oehmea nelsonii is a native of South Mexico; one is not surprised to read that it is rare. It is amazing that it manages to survive at all. The bright yellow flowers are said to be large and solitary. Presumably this is the reason for the original classification under *Dolichothele*.

Rapicactus

The two species of *Rapicactus* were formerly known as *Thelocactus subterraneus* and *Thelocactus mandragorus*. *R. subterraneus* has a round turnip-like root, with a long slender neck. A small, spiny globular cactus sits on top. The flowers are white. *R. mandragorus* also has a thick turnip-like root, and a very spiny globular stem, with whitish flowers. These plants are said to be difficult in cultivation, and are probably equally difficult to obtain.

Thelocactus

Thelocactus are found mainly in Mexico, but spread as far north as southern Texas. There are around 30 species. The ribs of these plants are divided into wide tubercles, and the large flowers are carried on top. These flowers are said to be spectacular, but we have never had any success in flowering the plants. We think we can safely say that they do not flower as young specimens.

Thelocactus bicolor is the species more frequently offered for sale. Although Borg describes the species as solitary, our specimen produced off-sets when about 6 cm. ($2\frac{1}{4}$ in.) across. The plant is said to reach a diameter of 10 cm. (4 in.). The bright red colour of the spines makes it very attractive even out of flower. There are 9–18 radials; these are red with amber-coloured tips. The 4 centrals are similarly coloured. The flowers are violet-red. Variety *tricolor* is a densely spined plant; the spines are red and white.

T. hexaedrophorus is a globular species, about 15 cm. (6 in.) high.

It has 6–9 radials which are yellow, gradually changing to a brown colour. The single central spine is also brown. The flowers are white.

T. lophothele is a clustering plant whose stems may reach a height of 25 cm. (10 in.). There are 3–5 amber coloured radials and only 1 central. The flowers are yellow, the petals having a red midrib.

T. nidulans has an almost globular stem about 20 cm. (8 in.) across and bluish-grey in colour, with wool at the top, and up to 15 stout brown spines to each areole. The flowers, when produced, are pale yellow and about 4 cm. (1½ in.) long.

EIGHT

Cacti of South America

South America is a great treasure house of cacti; all the small globular plants which flower so freely in our collections come from the Southern Hemisphere. Enormous areas of this continent are still unexplored and botanical searchers, such as F. Ritter, are discovering many beautiful plants every year.

Not only are the explorers and collectors busy south of the Panama Canal, the taxonomists are also hard at work! Plants move in and out of genera with great rapidity. We are on the side of simplicity; the fewer genera the better. But we are resigned to the fact that anything we now write will probably be out of date in a few years' time. With the death of Backeberg, who was a great creator of small genera, those botanists who felt that he went too far will no doubt try to simplify the naming of many cacti.

Acanthocalycium

The *Acanthocalycium* were at one time included in the genus *Echinopsis*. In our experience, they are less robust than the latter. They are inclined to lose their roots more readily if overwatered, and in prolonged periods of dull weather their buds will abort. The flowers lack the heavy scent of many of the echinopsis, and are smaller. Acanthocalyciums occur in the highlands of Argentina and, if kept completely dry in the winter, are hardy. There are at least 6 species, the best known being *A. klimpelianum, A. spiniflorum*, and *A. violaceum*.

A. klimpelianum is a globular plant, dark green in colour and about 10 cm. (4 in.) across. The areoles carry brownish curved spines, about 4 cm. (1½ in.) in length. *A. chionanthum* is similar, but has larger flowers.

A. spiniflorum is potentially a large plant; the dark green stem has been known to reach a height of 60 cm. (2 ft.) and 15 cm. (6 in.) across. The numerous needle-like spines are reddish-brown and the pink flowers are 4 cm. (1½ in.) long.

A. violaceum is a globular plant, reaching up to 12 cm. (4¾ in.) diameter. The yellow spines are stiff and bristly, and the pale violet flowers about 5 cm. (2 in.) across. Borg calls this plant *Echinopsis violacea.*

Two other species of acanthocalycium are *A. thionantum* and *A. formosum.* The latter has yellow flowers; we have had a large specimen for some years but have never flowered it.

Arthrocereus

Arthrocereus are not commonly seen in cultivation. Three species are described, all natives of Brazil. They are small prostrate plants with spiny stems, woody turnip-like roots, and large flowers, white or pale pink in colour. The most attractive-sounding species is *A. microsphaericus.* This is a prostrate plant; the stems consist of a series of spiny, rounded joints, about the size of an olive. The white flowers are sweetly scented.

Austrocactus

This is another genus which very few of us have seen in the flesh; the plants are natives of Patagonia and Argentina. They are low-growing, with stems about 6 cm. (2¼ in.) high and 3 cm. (1¼ in.) thick. The ribs are warty and the areoles are furnished with strongly hooked central spines. The flowers are pinkish. There are probably 2 species, *A. bertinii* and *A. dusenii.* It is possible that the latter plant is a variety of *A. bertinii.* The Zürich catalogue also lists *A. philippii.*

Brasilicactus   *See* Notocactus

Cacti of South America

Chamaecereus

Chamaecereus silvestrii is found growing among low bushes in western Argentina. All the numerous plants sold by nurseries in this country are descended from one clone imported from Argentina long ago. That is why, even if there are several specimens in a collection, obtained from different sources, *C. silvestrii* does not set seed; they are really all the same plant. Some botanists consider this cactus to be a *Lobivia*, but the name *Chamaecereus* is so well known that we retain it here.

A well-grown chamaecereus has short, finger-like, freely offsetting stems. These are prostrate, pale green, and covered with short white spines. During a good summer, the stems become violet in colour. The large scarlet flowers open around May or June. This plant is a problem at repotting time as it is impossible not to break off some of the stems. These loose shoots can be potted up and will soon form a new clump.

Chamaecerei have been crossed with lobivias to give large-flowered hybrids. These lack the vigour and free flowing habit of *C. silvestrii*. Chamaecerei will not cross with just any lobivia; we have tried cross-pollinating our plant with whatever lobivia happened to be in flower. The first time we tried, although seed was produced, it failed to germinate; the second time it germinated, but all the seedlings were chlorotic; there was no chlorophyll in any of them. We had not attempted any grafting at that time, or we might have been able to rear a few.

Provided the plant is kept dry, *C. silvestrii* will survive in an unheated greenhouse. To flower well this cactus needs a cold winter rest and plenty of sun. Chamaecerei grown in a poor light become distorted beyond recognition; a glance at many an office window-ledge will disclose a selection of etiolated cacti, among which is often a chamaecereus with long, weedy shoots.

There is a chlorotic form of chamaecereus, *C. silvestrii lutea*. If you like abnormal plants, the bright yellow stems have a certain fascination. Since this plant is without chlorophyll, it is unable to manufacture its own food and is a parasite on its graft. These plants are not cheap, and there is always the unpleasant possibility of the stock rotting at some inconvenient moment, such as the middle of December. If you buy one of these plants, and it is grafted on to *Myrtillocactus geometrizans*, as these plants often are, it is advisable to re-graft on to something hardier, such as a trichocereus.

Chileorebutia

The name *Chileorebutia* is invalid, these plants being now called *Thelocephala*, but the reader is quite likely to come across the former name in his reading. The important thing to remember is that they are not rebutias that happen to grow in Chile. The authorities Donald and Rowley consider that this genus should be lumped with *Neoporteria*, and we shall consider it in that section.

Copiapoa

Copiapoa have been known to botanists since the early part of the 19th century, but like many other globular cacti, they were disguised as *Echinocactus*. It is only recently, due to explorations of F. Ritter, that copiapoas have become better known. From being a small, obscure South American genus, they have become a large and popular one.

These plants are found on the northern coast of Chile, one of the most arid regions of the world. The main source of moisture is the winter mists. Many of the copiapoas are protected from the burning summer sun by a waxy coating.

Seedling copiapoas have tubercles which coalesce into ribs as the plants grow older. Many species have long tap-roots and mature specimens may form clusters.

The flowers are yellowish-white to deep yellow in colour, and have a very short tube. They are formed in the deep wool on top of the plant. Readers who grow *Wigginsia* will be familiar with flowers growing from a woolly crown. Copiapoas are difficult to flower in some areas; however, a few growers have been successful with *C. humilis* and *C. montana*. Cactus collectors in New Zealand seem to be able to flower young specimens quite easily. Copiapoas may need more sun than is available in this country to stimulate bud formation.

We have grown copiapoas successfully from seed. They are

not fast growing, but the seedlings are beautifully coloured and often heavily spined.

C. cinerea is a globular plant which becomes columnar with age and often clusters from the base. The skin is chalky white in colour and the spines black. The American botanist, Paul Hutchison, has found that the appearance of *C. cinerea* varies with its habitat. Those at high altitudes are globular, solitary and well-spined, whilst the coastal forms are columnar, branched and weakly-spined. These have been unjustifiably elevated to specific rank as *C. ferox, C. haseltonia, C. lembckei* and *C. brunnescens*.

C. krainziana is considered by many to be the most beautiful of this genus. It is certainly one of the best and most distinct, with its soft curly, hair-like spines. The epidermis is olive-green in colour. There is no record to date of this plant having flowered in cultivation.

C. marginata is one of the columnar species; it is greyish-green with woolly areoles and brown spines.

C. montana is a globular plant, greyish-green in colour with fine black spines.

Digitorebutia   Re-classified as *Rebutia* by Donald

Discocactus

Among the more 'touchy' cacti in cultivation we can include the *Discocactus*. These are globular plants with a cephalium on top, rather like a small melocactus and, like the latter, they need a minimum temperature of 13 °C (55 °F). These plants should be grown in a very open compost in full sun. They are definitely for the experienced grower and, we suspect, for the grower with a fair amount of money to spend.

Discocacti are native to Brazil, Paraguay and Bolivia. The number of species seems to be controversial, but is not above seven. In appearance they are globular plants with many ribs and stout spines. The large, scented flowers are usually white, and arise from the cephalium. They open at dusk and collapse before dawn. The seeds are large and, if fresh, germinate well; the young plants are said to grow strongly. Since plants raised from native seed are easier to cultivate than imported specimens, anyone with a warm greenhouse could well try these interesting cacti.

Echinopsis

Echinopsis have some of the most beautiful flowers in the *Cactaceae* family, but because they are easy to grow and hybridise, they are not as popular amongst collectors as they deserve to be. Many of the plants sold as species by nurseries are hybrids; very beautifully flowering plants, but nobody really wants his greenhouse filled with numerous very similar echinopsis of obscure parentage. However, habitat-collected seed is easily available and seedlings grow rapidly.

Echinopsis are hardy cacti, usually producing off-sets freely. We find that if kept dry they can survive the winter without heat. In our experience, echinopsis, when grown in pots, produce either flowers or off-sets. We remove the latter when about 1·5 cm. (just over ½ in.) in diameter (large enough to root) and we have little difficulty in flowering these plants. But echinopsis usually need to be about 8 cm. (3 in.) across before flowering. Fortunately they grow rapidly; we feed them during the flowering period.

The great homeland of many echinopsis is Argentina. However, recent explorations in Bolivia have added to the number of echinopsis species. We have found that these newer Bolivian plants are less tolerant of overwatering than the old-established species. If treated carelessly they may well lose their roots.

When reading through a catalogue one often comes across *Echinopsis 'x'*, then on another page *Pseudolobivia 'x'*, or perhaps it is *Echinopsis 'y'* and *Pseudoechinopsis 'y'*. It is rather disappointing to order an echinopsis and a pseudolobivia, only to find that they are one and the same plant. We are following Buxbaum here, who considers that *Echinopsis, Pseudolobivia* and *Pseudoechinopsis* should be united under *Echinopsis*. The pseudolobivias include some carmine-flowered species, and the pseudoechinopsis have bright yellow flowers instead of the more usual white or pink ones.

E. aurea has an elongated stem up to 10 cm. (4 in.) high, sprouting freely. The exquisite yellow flowers are about 9 cm. (3½ in.) long.

E. calorubra is from Bolivia where it is found at an altitude of 1,900 m. (6,300 ft.). It is a flattened globular plant about 7 cm. (2¾ in.) high and 14 cm. (5½ in.) across. The flowers are 15 cm. (6 in.) long and are orange-red in colour, with a magenta throat.

E. comarapana is yet another Bolivian cactus, growing at about 2,000 m. (6,600 ft.). It is a solitary, globular plant, about 15 cm. (6 in.) across. It is noted for the large numbers of its white flowers, often opening 10 at once.

E. eyriesii has been in cultivation for so long that it is often hybridised. Any white echinopsis tends to be labelled '*E. eyriesii*', but collected seed is available. It is a globular, clustering plant with spines ½ cm. (¼ in.) long, and sweetly scented white flowers about 25 cm. (10 in.) long.

E. hamatacantha is usually a solitary plant, and flowers when no more than 5 cm. (2 in.) across. Eventually it reaches a diameter of about 15 cm. (6 in.). The white flowers are small for an echinopsis, about 9 cm. (3½ in.) long.

E. kermesina is one of the carmine-flowered species. This has to be at least 6 cm. (2¼ in.) across before it produces its long-tubed flowers; they are unscented. The plant is globular, with many ribs, and rather long ginger spines. Our specimen has never clustered.

E. multiplex has sweetly scented, pale pink flowers, about 20 cm. (8 in.) long. The genuine species has long thick spines, but many plants, with pink flowers, sold as *E. multiplex*, have very short spines, and are obviously crosses with *E. eyriesii*.

E. rhodotricha is one of the largest species, eventually making a column 80 cm. (32 in.) high. Borg describes it as clustering, although our specimen has remained solitary. The flowers are about 15 cm. (6 in.) long, but only 8 cm. (3 in.) across. They are of a dull white colour, lacking the translucence that most echinopsis flowers have. They are scentless.

Echinopsis are closely related to lobivias, in fact some botanists would classify the latter as a sub-genus of the former. *Lobivia* × *Echinopsis* hybrids have the large flowers of the echinopsis, with the brilliant colours of the lobivias. These hybrids are usually closer to one parent than the other. Some are sweetly scented and open in the evening, typical echinopsis. Others are unscented and partially open in the evening, but do not fully open until the following morning. They are rather like large flowered lobivias. An echinopsis does not completely open until it is dark, but they can be fooled; 10 minutes in a dark cupboard and they open up fully. Echinopsis, like lobivias, usually have faded by the following evening.

The first echinobivias (or lobiviopsis as these hybrids are sometimes called), we grew were 'Green Gold' and 'Golden Dream', which were produced by Howard Gates in the United States. They both have long tubed, bright yellow flowers, which are slightly scented. The flowers are smaller than those of the species echinopsis. 'Green Gold' is almost spineless and off-sets freely. 'Golden Dream' has longer spines and produces off-sets less freely. Both are vigorous growers.

The most beautiful hybrids are the Johnson 'Paramount' hybrids. The first one we grew was 'Peach Monarch', with a large, satiny, peach-coloured flower. This plant unfortunately does not readily form off-sets, although it is a vigorous grower. An even more beautiful hybrid is 'Terracotta', having a huge, scented flower of a pearly pink colour with a deeper salmon mid-stripe down each petal. The spines are very short. Off-sets are freely produced. Other beautiful echinobivias are 'Aurora', large salmon-pink flowers with a yellow throat, 'Red Paramount' and 'Tangerine'. This last plant has pale orange flowers and is more like its lobivia parent. Although the flowers are small they are produced in profusion. Many of these echinobivias, although vigorous, do not readily form off-sets. However, we behead our plants. The top is easily re-rooted and the base, having lost its growing point, sprouts freely.

Eriocactus   *See* Notocactus

Frailea

When we first started growing cacti, we thought that *Frailea* had received their name because of their small size. Since then we have been disillusioned; they were named after Fraile, a curator of cacti in the U.S. Department of Agriculture. These plants have been known since 1838 (needless to say they were called '*Echinocactus*') and about 20 species have been described. Backeberg divided them into two groups, those without tubercles *(Frailea castanea)* and those with tubercles. This latter group was subdivided into three sections: cylindrical stems, semi-cylindrical stems, and globular stems.

Fraileas are quite widely distributed, occurring in Argentina, Paraguay, Uruguay, and south-east Brazil. They are amongst the smallest of cacti; probably only *Blossfeldia* are smaller. They reach only about 4 cm. (1½ in.) across when mature. Fraileas are noted for their cleistogamous flowers (the flowers can form seed without opening). When conditions are right, they can open their flowers, but growers are uncertain just what the plant wants to stimulate opening. Sometimes they open on warm, sunny days, and then surprise their owners by opening during a dull, cloudy period. The flowers are carried on the tops of the plants, and the petals are yellow. One writer found that with *F. cataphracta* the flowers that opened produced about twice as many seeds as those that remained closed.

Fraileas are not difficult to cultivate on their own roots. They do best in an acidic soil, and should be grown in pans rather than individually in small pots.

F. caespitosa comes from Uruguay. It is rather elongate in shape, and clusters freely. There are short, yellowish radial spines and longer, curved centrals.

F. castanea is possibly the most attractive of the fraileas. It is like a miniature version of *Astrophytum asterias*, and was at one time known as *F. asteroides*. This native of south-east Brazil is grey-bronze in colour and about 4·5 cm. (1¾ in.) across.

F. cataphracta is one of the globular species and clusters freely. The heads are about 4 cm. (1½ in.) across at maturity. The many ribs are notched into small warts and each areole has a crescent-shaped brownish spot on its lower half.

F. gracillima is a cylindrical species and is slow growing with a tendency to lose its roots if overwatered. It will eventually make an olive green column about 10 cm. (4 in.) high, and clustering from the base.

F. knippeliana forms an elongated bright green plant about 4 cm. (1½ in.) high and 2–5 cm. (about 1 in.) thick. It does not cluster readily. The radial spines are short and curved, and the centrals slightly longer, up to 1 cm. (⅜ in.). The red and yellow streaked flowers open only in full sun.

Gymnocalycium

The genus *Gymnocalycium* is much more closely defined than many other genera of cacti. There may be differences of opinion amongst botanists about separation of species and varieties, but most specialists are agreed about which plants should be included in the genus. This is largely because gymnocalyciums have some definite characters which make their identification comparatively easy. A few botanists have attempted to include other genera with the gymnocalyciums, such as *Weingartia* and *Neowerdermannia,* but this has not been generally accepted in Europe. On the whole, since the genus was named in 1845, the conception of it has remained unchanged, although naturally further species have been discovered, reaching nearly a hundred at the present time.

The most important distinguishing characteristic of the gymnocalyciums, and the only really reliable one, is the smooth, naked flower buds and flower tubes. The scaly buds are quite easily recognised by any grower, who should have no difficulty in identifying a gymnocalycium when in bud. Another feature which can be seen in the plant when not in bud is the possession of a cleft below each tubercle, giving a 'chin-like' effect. This is not absolutely characteristic as a few other cacti, notably some neoporteria, also show it, whilst some gymnocalyciums almost lose their chins in cultivation.

Gymnocalyciums are mostly globular plants with comparatively few ribs, divided into tubercles. The 'chin' is produced by a protuberance of the tubercle below the areole, with a cleft beneath it. Spine length and shape vary greatly with the species, some of which have short, thin spines, whilst others possess long, stout, curved ones. This variation of spine formation adds to the attractiveness of these plants even when out of flower. They

125

mostly flower readily, some species when quite young plants. The flowering season starts in spring and reaches a maximum in June and July, and some species will continue through until autumn. The flowers are usually quite large, about 5 cm. (2 in.) across, and last for several days. Most species appear to be self-sterile and seed is not usually produced unless cross-pollination has taken place.

The cultivation of gymnocalyciums presents no special difficulties; a well-drained, fairly rich soil gives good results, and the usual cultivation recommended for cacti is all that is needed. These plants are quite accommodating in their need for light, and do not demand the sunniest part of the greenhouse, although, in our experience, there is no need to shade them deliberately, at least not in our area. They are quite easily raised from seed. Their native habitats are mostly the higher ground of Argentina and Paraguay, the eastern lower slopes of the Andes, and part of Patagonia. An important area is southern Bolivia, with many excellent species.

Gymnocalyciums are ideal plants for a specialist collection, and their varied spine formation and flowers make at least a few essential for the general collector. There is, unfortunately, a snag! Nurserymen and others who compile plant catalogues have allowed their enthusiasm to exceed their accuracy, and many of these cacti that have been described by botanists as varieties are often listed as 'species'. This leads to some confusion amongst collectors and it is all too easy to buy the same, or almost the same, gymnocalycium under several different names. The only way to avoid this is to know of the recognised species and their varieties, and we have included a list of some of these in the hope that a few readers at least will not be 'caught out', as we have been in the past!

The following includes most of the main types of gymno-calyciums; many others are either varieties or very similar.

G. andreae is a most desirable species in that it is small growing, reaching a diameter of under 5 cm. (2 in.), and freely produces bright yellow flowers (an unusual colour for this genus). These flowers are about 3 cm. (1¼ in.) across. Off-sets are freely produced on our plants.

G. asterium (syn. *G. stellatum*) has white flowers and is particularly easily raised from seed and flowered. *G. bodenbenderianum* is similar.

G. baldianum (syn. *G. venturianum*) reaches a diameter of about 7 cm. (3 in.). The usual flower colour is dark red but pink-flowered specimens sometimes occur. There are short, spreading radial spines and no centrals.

G. bruchii (syn. *G. lafaldense*) is another small, clump-forming species. The white flowers, tinged with pink, are freely produced. The spines are small.

G. cardenasianum is a Bolivian species, at the moment somewhat a rarity, but specimens are becoming available. It does not flower readily, but has most attractive stout, curved spines. The flower is pink and quite large.

G. damsii is a plant very similar to *G. mihanovichii*, and flowers when quite small. We have flowered seedlings when about 2 cm. ($\frac{3}{4}$ in.) across. It grows well from seed and has most attractive striped markings. The spines are small and bristle-like, and the flowers pale pink, or white. There are several varieties.

G. denudatum is the type species of the genus *Gymnocalycium* and comes from southern Brazil, Uruguay, Paraguay and Argentina. The plant may be up to 10 cm. (4 in.) high and 15 cm. (6 in.) across, with spreading radial spines and no centrals. The flowers are large and mainly white.

G. gibbosum had originally many varieties, reduced by Backeberg to three. It may reach 8 cm. (3 in.) diameter. Variety *nigrum* is particularly attractive with fairly stout black spines. The flowers are white or reddish. The other varieties are *leucodictyon* and *nobilis*.

G. leeanum from Uruguay is interesting since it is a dwarf cluster-ing species with yellow flowers, and is particularly easy from seed. The small radial spines lie close to the plant body; there are no centrals.

G. mihanovichii is a variable species with many varieties (see list). It has well-defined ribs and the colour is greyish-green, often with reddish markings. The radial spines are up to about 1 cm. ($\frac{3}{8}$ in.) long and curved. There are no centrals. The plant reaches a diameter of about 5 cm. (2 in.) but flowers freely when much smaller. The flowers are typically greenish-yellow, but may be pink or yellowish.

127

G. mihanovichii var. *friedrichii* has a cultivar, 'Ruby Ball'. This, also known as 'Hibotan', was introduced from Japan. It is bright red in colour, and as it contains no chlorophyll must always be grown grafted. Another cultivar is 'Hibotan Nishiki', with green and red stripes. This is much rarer at the moment, but requires the same treatment. These plants do not flower readily. The Japanese stock used is *Myrtillocactus geometrizans*; this is very susceptible to rot in damp winters and is often lost. We would advise the purchaser of one of these plants to re-graft on to a trichocereus.

G. monvillei is a most attractive species even out of flower. The long, stout spines are pale yellow, with red at the base. They are all radials. The flowers are white or pale pink.

G. mostii has long, stout central spines, slightly curved, and one straight central. The flower is pink.

G. multiflorum is a strong growing plant with stout spines. Despite the name, it is rather less free-flowering than most of this genus. The flowers, when produced, are whitish.

G. platense has spreading radial spines and whitish flowers with a green tinge, and red at the base of the petals.

G. leptanthum is very similar to the above, but with shorter flower tubes. These two plants are often confused.

G. pungens has long, stout, almost straight spines. It is quite a recent species, having been named only in 1962, but seed is available here. The flower is white, but the plant is very attractive with dark markings on deep green.

G. quehlianum is a white-flowered species somewhat similar to *G. platense*. A hybrid of these two plants is sometimes listed as '*G. henissii*'.

G. saglionis is another species with long, stout spines. These are usually dark in colour and curved. It does not usually flower when small, but makes an impressive plant, reputed to reach a diameter of 30 cm. (1 ft.) in the wild.

G. schickendantzii is an attractive plant with slightly spiral ribs and well-defined tubercles. The spines are stout and slightly curved, brown or grey with dark tips. The greenish flowers are about 5 cm. (2 in.) long. *G. delaetii* is very similar.

The following varieties of *Gymnocalycium* species are sometimes listed by dealers as 'species'.

Cacti of South America

Dealer's name	Variety of:
G. backebergii	*G. denudatum*
G. caespitosum	*G. gibbosum*
G. delaetianum	*G. denudatum*
G. ferox	*G. gibbosum*
,,	*G. hybopleurum*
,,	*G. mazanense*
G. fleischerianum	*G. mihanovichii*
G. melocactiforme	*G. mihanovichii*
G. paraguayense	*G. denudatum*
G. pirarettaense	*G. mihanovichii*
G. stenogonum	*G. mihanovichii*
G. tilcarense	*G. saglionis*
G. zantnerianum	*G. quelianum*

Gymnocalycium leonense is the same as *G. chubutense*, which is a valid species but very similar to *G. gibbosum*. Some plants sold as *G. delaetianum* may be *G. delaetii*, closely related to *G. schickendantzii*. This adds to the confusion, but only emphasises the fact that one must take great care when ordering gymnocalyciums from a dealer's list!

Islaya

The first *Islaya* was discovered in 1861 and named *Echinocactus islayensis*. About 50 years later, a second species was found, '*Malococarpus islayensis*' this time. In 1931 Backeberg discovered a further species, and created the genus *Islaya*. Since then many islayas have been named, mainly by Hoffman, Rauh and Ritter. At the moment the count stands at about 14 species, but at least one authority, J. Donald, considers that they are all geographical variants of *I. islayensis*, and this itself a species of *Neoporteria*.

Islayas are found growing along the Pacific coast of Chile, Ecuador and Peru. This is a region of almost no rainfall. The main source of moisture is the 'garua' or mist caused by the icy Humboldt current. This mist is carried inland as a blanket of cloud by the penetrating wind. The plants grow amongst pebbles and are almost buried in the soil. This of course makes them very hard to find and explains the reason for islayas being so little known until recently. They have particularly shallow roots to deal with this surface water, and some moisture may be absorbed through their spines and epidermis.

In appearance islayas are globular or cylindrical and apparently solitary. There is much 'wool' on top of the plant and the yellow flowers are produced from this. The plants are well armed with stout spines. There is considerable variation in size from *I. minor*, which is about 10 cm. (4 in.) high, to *I. grandis*, about 50 cm. (20 in.) high and 20 cm. (8 in.) across. The tallest species is *I. krainziana* about 12 cm. (5 in.) across and up to 75 cm. (30 in.) high. *I. brevicylindrica* grows at Camana in sight of the Pacific Ocean. The closely packed radial spines and dark, curved centrals give the thick stems a very attractive appearance. The flowers are yellowish and in cultivation are produced on plants about 6 cm. (2½ in.) tall.

These cacti are very slow growing. We have had no experience in their cultivation ourselves, but experienced growers recommend a very gritty compost and only occasional waterings. They should be sprayed on sunny days. The important thing is to grow islayas as near to the glass as possible; they need all the light available.

Lobivia

Lobivia are very closely related to *Echinopsis* and intergeneric hybrids are in cultivation (see echinobivia under *Echinopsis*). It has been suggested that *Lobivia* is a subgenus of *Echinopsis*. Whatever their name, lobivias are beautiful plants, easy to cultivate, and easily raised from seed.

Lobivias are found growing on the slopes of the Andes in Argentina, Bolivia and Peru (the name is an anagram of Bolivia). They grow at altitudes of between 2,500 m. and 4,500 m. (8,000 to 15,000 ft.). The temperature in this region drops to −15 °C (5 °F), but it should be remembered that the plants are completely dry. Lobivias are often found deeply embedded in the soil, or hidden by other vegetation and rocks; this helps to hide them from the hungry eyes of goats and llamas, who will eat anything that is green and juicy.

In appearance, lobivias are small, frequently clustering plants, and often have extensive tuberous roots. Some species have to be grown in comparatively large pots to house a long turnip-like tap-root. Many lobivias have strong spines and even hair which, it has been suggested, insulates them against the winter cold. Even if the spines fail to keep the plants warm, they may to some extent discourage the goats.

The funnel-shaped flowers are up to 10 cm. (4 in.) across. They are diurnal and brightly coloured in shades of red, purple, orange, yellow, pink and white. Unfortunately they are short-lived and in hot weather usually last only one day.

The naming of lobivias is confused due to the large variation amongst individual species. Also many of the plants in cultivation are hybrids. We shall describe some of the main groups.

Amongst the plants which grow farthest north are *Lobivia tegeleriana* and the similar *L. oyonica, L. insularis* and *L. westii.* Their flowers vary from yellow to red. Also in this area are found the *L. hertrichiana* 'group', including *L. allegraiana, L. minuta* and *L. planiceps. L. hertrichiana*, with its dark red flowers and freely clustering habit, is often to be seen in collections.

Coming further south, we meet the *L. pentlandii* complex. *L. pentlandii* was the first lobivia described and has numerous forms. Borg lists 18 varieties, differing from the type plant in flower colour (orange, yellow, red and pink) and also in spination. *L. pentlandii* itself is a clustering plant with red flowers. Included in this complex are *L. higginsiana* (dark red flowers) and *L. leuco-violacea* (white).

Lobivia cinnabarina is often listed in catalogues. This is a cylindrical plant which clusters with age. The flowers are a glowing red. Included in this group are *L. acanthopligma, L. rossii* and *L. waltherspielii.*

Some of the most beautiful flowers are found in the *L. jajoiana* group. *L. jajoiana* itself is a short cylindrical plant which forms an occasional off-set. The flowers are deep red with a black throat. In this group are *L. fleischeriana* and *L. vatteri.*

In a few lines we can only scratch the surface of the lobivia problem. We have come reluctantly to the conclusion that most of our own plants do not match the names on their labels! With lobivias, perhaps there is much to be said for not worrying too much about their names, but for growing them simply for the beauty of their flowers.

Matucana

The genus *Matucana* is named after the town of Matucana in the mountains of Peru. Dr Rose collected specimens of *Echinocactus haynei* (this was first described in 1850 when most spherical cacti were called *Echinocactus*) from the neighbourhood of Matucana and named the genus after the place where it was collected. Recently other botanists have discovered more species of matucanas in the valleys around this town.

The young specimens of matucanas that most of us possess are globular, and it is only after many years that they become cylindrical. The young plants are extremely beautiful, some species being covered with dense silvery spines. The long, slender flowers are zygomorphic and most commonly red in colour.

The only matucana that we have seen in bloom in this country is *M. aurantiaca*; mature specimens of matucanas are not common in collections. *M. aurantiaca* has a deep green stem with brownish spines, and the flower is a deep yellow, with a trace of orange on some of the petals.

M. crinifera is frequently seen as young specimens. It is a very beautiful plant, the stem being completely hidden by the soft, silvery spines.

M. haynei eventually makes a plant about 60 cm. (2 ft.) high and 10 cm. (4 in.) across. On young plants, the spines are shining white and completely hide the epidermis. The flowers are red.

M. yanganucensis makes an attractive seedling; the stem is densely covered with creamy-fawn spines.

Mediolobivia   Now included under *Rebutia*

Mila

Mila is an anagram of Lima, and these small cacti are natives of Peru. They have cylindrical stems which branch from the base, and the small yellow flowers are carried on top. Some writers claim that milas are easy to grow; perhaps we have not the art of mila growing because we have found them rather prone to rot. *M. caespitosa* is a prostrate plant with stems about 3 cm. (1¼ in.)

thick and 15 cm. (6 in.) long. The numerous spines are brownish. *M. kubeana* and *M. nealeana* are very similar to *M. caespitosa. M. pugionifera* is the species most often seen in plant lists. The stem is erect.

Neoporteria

The present genus *Neoporteria* includes a number of former genera. Donald and Rowley have suggested that it should include *Thelocephala (Chileorebutia), Horridocactus, Nichelia (Neochilenia), Pyrrocactus, Reichocactus* and *Islaya*. The original *Neoporteria* have rose-mauve coloured flowers, with purple stigmas, whilst the more recently included genera have pale yellow or rose flowers and cream or pink stigmas. The genus currently contains about 66 species.

Neoporterias are found in the Andes of Argentina and Peru. As young plants they are globular, but become cylindrical with age. We have found that, with a few exceptions, they grow well on their own roots. Grafting is said to have an odd effect on plants of *N. reichii*; they appear to become elongated and grafted specimens have reached 1 m. (39 in.) in length. This is partially confirmed by our grafted seedling which is now five times as long as it is wide, and still elongating.

Neoporterias flower easily, the flowers being carried on the top of the plants. Those with cream flowers bloom in early summer, whilst the purple-flowered species (the original neoporterias) open their buds in October. These late-flowering species come into growth after many other cacti and continue growing well into the autumn. They should be watered accordingly.

Most of the neoporterias we have grown have remained solitary. The only exception is a grafted plant sold to us as *N. taltalensis* which 'pups' as freely as an echinopsis. But this may be an abnormality due to grafting.

Since neoporterias are high-altitude plants we have tried growing them without heat. They survived but developed ugly brown marks.

Many neoporterias have beautiful dark brown skins. One of these which we have found particularly easy to flower is the purple-flowered *N. densispina. N. wagenknechtii* also produces its purple flowers when small, but the plant body is bright green and less attractive. All these species are well spined.

Among the cream-flowered species is *N. taltalensis* with a dark brown epidermis and dark spines. We find (always assuming that our plant is correctly named) that this is particularly free-flowering, giving several flushes of bloom during the summer. *N. esmeraldana* also has yellowish flowers but is said to be less easy to flower than the above. However, its beautiful violet-red body makes it a highly desirable addition to any collection.

This plant, together with *N. duripulpa*, was originally in the genus *Chileorebutia*, now named *Thelocephala* and included under *Neoporteria* in the most recent classification. These former *Chileorebutia* are small plants, and if grown on their own roots, must have a very porous compost. They are frequently sold grafted, when their rate of growth is somewhat faster.

N. hankeana is an easily grown plant with a green stem and stout spines. The flowers are cream.

N. jussieui is a species with pale pink flowers. The body is dark and the spines about 2·5 cm. (1 in.) long.

Neowerdermannia

N. vorwerkii is found at heights of up to 5,000 m. (15,000 ft.) in Bolivia. It is a globular plant, about 8 cm. (3 in.) across, and with a thick, turnip-like root. The spines are brownish, spreading star-like from the areoles. The flower is white with a lilac midrib to the petals.

Notocactus

Notocactus are found in the grasslands of South America, and in our experience these plants are vigorous, hardy, and easy to flower. The only exception we have come across is *N. schumannianus*; this plant does not seem to have the resistance to cold of the other species. We have killed at least two specimens, whilst all our other notocacti have flourished despite their unheated cold frame in winter, and sometimes being overwatered in summer. Most notocacti will flower when very young. The large flowers are carried on top of the plant, and are most commonly yellow with purple-red stigmas; usually self-fertile. The seed germinates easily and the young plants grow rapidly.

Like many other genera, the notocactus classification is under review. Many new areas of South America are being opened up, beautiful new species of notocacti are being collected and old species are being rediscovered in the wild. Many of the plants in cultivation bear little resemblance to the type plant, and other 'species' should probably be reduced to varietal status.

Backeberg separated from the genus *Notocactus* two other genera, *Brasilicactus* and *Eriocactus*. The plants left in *Notocactus* were globular, with yellow flowers having a purplish stigma. *Brasilicactus* were globular with small red or green flowers and yellow stigmas. *Eriocactus* were cylindrical plants with yellow flowers and stigmas. Since Backeberg's classification, whole colonies of plants have been examined and it has been found that some have purple stigmas whilst their neighbours have yellow ones. Also specimens have been found intermediate between *Notocactus* and *Brasilicactus*. Botanists now consider that these genera should be re-united under *Notocactus*.

There are three species of *Notocactus* which were once in the genus *Brasilicactus*:

N. elachisanthus is not common in cultivation.

N. graessneri has golden-yellow spines and small green flowers. The buds are a beautiful emerald green. Some specimens have spines of a deeper colour than others. The growing centre is sometimes to one side of the plant.

N. haselbergii is a pure white ball with tomato red flowers. In our experience these species do not flower as young plants.

N. leninghausii is the most notable member of Backeberg's genus, *Eriocactus*. This is a golden plant which branches and becomes columnar with age. The large yellow flowers are not borne on young specimens. As with *N. graessneri*, the growing centre tends to be on one side of the stem.

N. schumannianus is globular as a young plant but becomes cylindrical with age, and may reach a length of over 1 m. (39 in.). The new spines are reddish-brown, discolouring when older. The flowers are yellow.

Among the more recent discoveries in the *Eriocactus* group of *Notocactus* are *N. claviceps* and *N. magnificus*. The former is a cylindrical plant, similar to *N. schumannianus*, but only reaches a height of about 50 cm. (20 in.), whilst *N. magnificus* is also cylindrical with golden-yellow spines, and branching from the base. The yellow flowers are about 5 cm. (2 in.) across. This species was discovered as recently as 1964 by Horst and Ritter.

With the species of notocacti that have been in cultivation for a long time, it is necessary to proceed with caution. Most of us have probably never seen a genuine *N. apricus*. There is a group of globular plants with large yellow flowers bearing names such as *N. apricus*, *N. concinnus*, *N. muricatus*, and *N. tabularis*. These cacti are solitary and densely covered with soft spines in shades of yellow and brown. They flower when quite small and appear to be self-fertile.

Another group of plants is centred around *N. mammulosus*. In addition to this species there are *N. pampeanus* and *N. submammulosus*. *N. floricomus* and its varieties are closely related. These are also globular, solitary plants, but their spines are longer and stouter, looking more prickly than the preceding group. The spines are usually brownish, but *N. floricomus* has a variety with deep red spines. The flowers are a little smaller than those of the ʽ*apricus*' group, and seed is set freely.

N. ottonis is quite different from most of the other notocacti; it is a small globular plant which clusters freely. The yellow flowers are very large, about 6 cm. (2¼ in.) across. There are many varieties of this species.

N. scopa is also an unmistakable species with many varieties. The most commonly seen plant is *N. s.* var. *ruberrima*. This is pale green and globular (old plants elongate) and is covered with soft, silvery radial spines. The centrals are crimson; in the type species they are brown. An even more beautiful plant is *N. s.* var. *candida*, with white central spines. All these plants flower when small, the flowers are yellow. Our specimen of *N. s.* var. *candida* started to branch from along the stem when quite young; our other varieties have remained solitary.

We must now consider the new species of notocacti. With these, one is on much firmer ground, as most of the plants in cultivation are either imported or grown from habitat-collected stock. One of the results of the recent explorations in South America has been the discovery of many of these species, some

of which are greatly different from the species which we have
been growing for years. *N. bueneckeri*, along with *N. brevihamata*
and *N. alacriportanus*, were at first placed in the genus *Parodia*.
However, recent studies of the flower and fruit showed that these
were more closely related to *Notocactus*, and Buxbaum and
Krainz made the transfer. The original specimen of *N. bueneckeri* had long, thin, hooked spines and large yellow flowers, but
more recently forms have been discovered with smaller flowers
and shorter spines, which seem to merge with *N. alacriportanus*.
We have one of the short spined versions of *N. bueneckeri*; it
grows with a vigour which alone would make one doubt that it
was a parodia. It flowers early in the spring, before the other
species of notocacti.

N. crassigibbus, and the very similar *N. arachnites*, are the so-
called 'Gymnocalycoiid' notocacti, although in our opinion the
resemblance to gymnocalyciums is not very great. However, they
can be distinguished from gymnocalyciums by the position of
the areole, which is in the fold between the tubercles. In gymnocalyciums, it is on top of the tubercle. The flowers of these two
notocacti are the typical yellow ones of this genus, and they do
not have the naked, scaly buds of gymnocalyciums. Included in
this group is *N. ubelmannianus* with deep magenta flowers.

N. herteri is a globular plant with brownish-red spines. The large
flowers are light purple to deep magenta in colour.

N. horstii is a cylindrical plant with bright orange flowers which
are rather smaller than those of the above species. The spines
are brownish.

N. rauschii is globular and covered with needle-like spines, either
white or pale rose in colour. The large flowers are yellow.

N. rechensis is a small globular notocactus which sprouts from
the base. The spines are white or yellow in colour and the
flowers yellow.

Oroya

This genus gives some difficulty to taxonomists with regard to its
precise placing in the *Cactaceae*, and until quite recently the
plants were not easy to obtain. However, they are now much
more freely available, both as seed and imported plants. The

137

genus has a limited distribution in Peru where the plants are found at an altitude of 3,500–4,000 m. (11,000–13,000 ft.). The natural habitat is characterised by a wide range of day–night temperature and high winter humidity, but there are several months in summer which are very dry. In cultivation as much sun as possible should be given. Although these cacti do not appear to flower readily under conditions other than found in their natural habitat, they are nevertheless very beautiful plants, with their fine spines. Around 6 species are described, but the exact number is complicated by the presence of possible varieties.

O. borchersii is one of the most likely species to be met in cultivation. The plant body is globular, reaching a maximum diameter of 20 cm. (8 in.) and is covered with strong spines. The flowers are yellow.

O. peruviana is the type species, similar in appearance to the above, but it is very variable, particularly in spine colour. The flowers are reddish.

Parodia

When we first started collecting cacti, about 15 years ago, there were about 30 species of *Parodia* described in Borg. When it actually came to buying plants, most catalogues listed about two or three species. Since then the number of available species has increased enormously. Recent explorations in South America have not only increased the notocacti, but also the parodias. Seed is freely available and it would now be possible to fill a small greenhouse with these plants. There are said to be now over 90 species.

One reason for the shortage of parodias in plant catalogues is that they do not lend themselves to mass production. The seed is minute and initially the young seedlings are slow growing. After the first year growth speeds up; we have flowered our own seedlings.

Parodias are not the easiest of the cacti in cultivation. They have the unfortunate habit of losing their roots without any apparent reason. Usually they grow a new set and it is possible for a plant to lose and gain new roots without leaving any obvious mark on the stem. We have tried grafting one or two particularly difficult specimens, but have found that they have not even done very well grafted. However, it is possible to have a difficult plant, and when it finally dies to replace it with another of the same species which never gives any trouble.

It is not always possible to predict whether a particular parodia is going to be difficult, but we can name some species which we have grown easily; *P. aureispina, P. faustiana, P. gracilis, P. maassii suprema, P. mairanana,* and *P. mutabilis.* Anyone wishing to start a collection of parodias should find that these would make a good nucleus.

When we were new to the hobby of cactus collecting we believed whatever we read, namely that parodias were small, solitary plants with large flowers. With more experience behind us (not to mention dead plants!) we now know that some parodias become large. We have a *P. aureispina* about 20 cm. (8 in.) high and 12·5 cm. (5 in.) across. Many parodias form off-sets freely, and some of the new species have disappointingly small flowers.

With the parodias, many of the newly discovered species are certainly not better than the ones we have been growing for years. They tend to have small yellow flowers, and many have straight ribs instead of the spirally arranged ribs of the older species.

Most parodias are found in the eastern Andes of Bolivia and Argentina. Some of the stout-spined species, such as *P. maassii,* are found at altitudes of 4,000 m. (13,000 ft.). Unfortunately these heavily spined species appear to be difficult to flower. We owned a specimen of *P. maassii* for 10 years without a sign of a bud, although the plant was growing vigorously.

P. aureispina forms a large golden ball. The ribs are spirally arranged and the body is densely covered with short yellow spines; at least one of the centrals is hooked. The buttercup-yellow flowers are large and freely produced. Our own specimen is vigorous, and so far has not produced off-sets.

P. ayopayana is a cylindrical plant with straight ribs and pale brown spines, which are not numerous; the centrals are straight. The small flowers are apricot-yellow. Our specimen has formed some off-sets, and did not flower as a small plant.

P. chrysacanthion is a globular species with spirally arranged ribs and the pale green stem is covered with long light yellow spines; the centrals are straight. The yellow flowers are quite small.

This species is grown for the beauty of its spines rather than for its flowers.

P. echinus is probably a form of *P. gigantea*. It is a rapidly growing cylindrical plant with straight ribs and brownish spines. As with most of the straight-ribbed parodias, the spines are not numerous, and certainly do not cover the stem. The insignificant yellow flowers start to appear in February. Off-sets are formed.

P. faustiana is a particularly beautiful species, flowering when about 2·5 cm. (1 in.) across. The spirally arranged ribs carry numerous white spines, completely covering the stem. The large flowers are a copper colour.

P. gracilis is a pale green globular cactus with spirally arranged ribs and numerous white spines. The small flowers are apricot-yellow, but our specimen did not flower until about 5 cm. (2 in.) across.

P. maassii is a species with stout, curved, central spines; the radials are bristle-like. The ribs are spirally arranged and divided into rounded warts. As mentioned above, in our experience, this parodia does not flower readily, when it does, the flowers are brick-red.

P. maassii suprema is a vigorous plant with stout, dark brown spines. When we first saw the size of the spines, we thought we had another non-flowering plant. However, when about 5–8 cm. (2–3 in.) across, our plant produced medium-sized red flowers. It appears to be one of the more attractive of the newer species.

P. mairanana is a globular, freely sprouting plant. The ribs are straight and the short spines yellowish. The apricot flowers do not appear until mid-July, but the plant continues to flower until November.

P. mutabilis is a vigorous plant with spirally-arranged ribs, whitish radial spines and orange-yellow centrals. The large flowers are yellow.

P. nivosa is a very beautiful plant but one which we find difficult to keep. The stem is thickly covered with silvery-white spines, all of which are straight. The scarlet flowers are produced when the plant is about 2·5 cm. (1 in.) across.

P. ocampoi is a cylindrical plant with straight ribs and brown spines. It is characterised by a white woolly top in which are embedded ridiculously small red flowers. Despite the smallness of the flowers, the plant is about 8 cm. (3 in.) high before flowering.

P. sanguiniflora is a globular species with brownish spines and spiral ribs. The central spines are hooked. Numerous large dark crimson flowers are produced. Our specimen formed many off-sets which unfortunately had an adverse effect on the flowering, the flowers decreasing in number as the off-sets increased.

Pygmaeocereus

This genus was created in 1957 by Backeberg; the type plant is *P. bylesianus*, probably coming from Peru. It is a small plant, branching from the base, with stems about 10 cm. (4 in.) long. These stems have 12–14 ribs and the areoles many greyish spines. The slender white flowers, with a tube about 15 cm. (6 in.) long, are nocturnal. From the illustration included with the description of the plant, the flowers are carried just below the crown of the stem.

This genus is now generally united with *Arthrocereus*.

Rebutia

The genus *Rebutia* was at one time divided into numerous smaller genera, such as *Aylostera, Mediolobivia, Setirebutia,* and *Cylindrorebutia*. It has been suggested by Buining and Donald that these smaller units should be re-united under *Rebutia*. They go even further and reduce the total number of species. Recent studies on plants in the wild have shown that many of the former 'species' of rebutia are so closely related that they should be treated as varieties, or even colour forms.

Rebutias are small, usually freely clustering cacti found in Argentina and Bolivia. They are found at altitudes between 1,500 and 5,000 m. (4,800 and 16,000 ft.), growing amongst grass. We grow our plants with very little heat and they appear to thrive. Every spring we are treated to a mass of colour from the rebutias, even one-year-old seedlings. The funnel-shaped flowers are formed around the sides of the plant, arising from near the base (we had 72 flowers on one plant 7·5 cm. (3 in.) high). These flowers come in a variety of colours; red, orange, pink, yellow, mauve and white. Many of the rebutias grown are probably hybridised as these cacti set seed freely, but even obscure hybrids are beautiful. It is said that rebutias are short-lived compared with other cacti; certainly we have had plants which seemed to flower themselves to death. One of us has never been able to keep *R. minuscula* for more than three or four years. The plant reaches a diameter of about 5 cm. (2 in.), smothers itself with flowers, and then dries up. Fortunately rebutias are readily propagated from their off-sets, which root easily.

The rebutias most commonly grown are *R. minuscula*, *R. senilis* and *R. xanthocarpa*, and their forms and varieties. We shall deal with these first and then mention some of the newer and less common species. It is, however, important to remember that many rebutias sold as named plants often bear little resemblance to the type plant. Probably the best hope of obtaining some of the choice rebutias is to buy imported seed.

R. minuscula is a bright green, freely-clustering plant with short whitish spines. The red flowers are self-fertile.

R. minuscula forma *violaciflora* has short ginger spines and deep lilac-pink flowers.

R. minuscula var. *grandiflora* is a freely-clustering plant with red flowers which have exceptionally long tubes. The flowers reach above the plant body.

R. senilis is freely-clustering and covered with long white spines. The flowers are red and self-fertile.

R. senilis forma *lilacina-rosea* has lilac-pink flowers.

R. senilis var. *iseliniana* has very long orange-red flowers, and forma *kesselringiana* has smaller yellow flowers and light green buds. This distinguishes it easily from the yellow flowered *R. marsoneri*, with brown buds.

R. xanthocarpa is a caespitose plant, covered with short white spines. The red flowers are small and set seed freely.

R. xanthocarpa forma *salmonea* has small salmon-pink flowers.

Amongst the other rebutias are the following:

R. albiflora is a shortly-cylindrical, freely-clustering plant with individual heads, about 1 cm. ($\frac{3}{8}$ in.) across. All the specimens we have seen have been grafted, but can be grown on their own roots if kept warmer in winter. The short spines are white, as also are the flowers.

R. calliantha is one of the larger rebutias and is more cylindrical than most members of this genus, sometimes reaching a height of 15 cm. (6 in.). The spines are whitish and the very large flowers, up to 4·5 cm. (1¾ in.) across, are red. The buds are a deep purplish colour.

R. calliantha var. *beryllioides* has a bright green flattened body with yellow to golden-brown spines and bright scarlet flowers.

R. calliantha var. *krainziana* is a caespitose plant with short white spines and large red flowers.

R. deminuta is a clustering, shortly-cylindrical plant with brown spines and orange-red flowers.

R. fiebrigii is a shortly-cylindrical clustering plant, covered with numerous brownish spines. The flowers are orange-red.

R. haagei has numerous small, finger-like growths. The stems are purplish-brown, covered with small tubercles. The minute star-like spines are whitish, and the comparatively large flowers are salmon-pink.

R. kupperiana has a very dark green, almost bronze, stem. The short spines are brown, and the large flowers a deep orange-red.

R. marsoneri is a caespitose, light green plant with whitish spines. The brownish buds open to large golden-yellow flowers.

R. muscula, not to be confused with *R. minuscula,* is a caespitose plant covered with numerous soft white spines. The flowers are light orange-red.

R. pulvinosa is a shortly-cylindrical plant which sprouts freely. The short, slender spines are white and the small flowers orange.

R. rubiginosa is a dark green plant with rust-coloured spines. This species does not off-set freely. The flowers are intense vermilion.

R. tuberosa is a many-headed clump, arising from a turnip-like rootstock. The heads are hemispherical and dark green in colour, with yellowish-brown spines, not numerous, and the flowers are vermilion.

Sulcorebutia

The *Sulcorebutia,* despite their name, are more closely related to *Lobivia* and *Weingartia* than to *Rebutia*. In 1931 Werderman described a '*Rebutia steinbachii*' and commented on the combination of rebutia-like flowers on a lobivia-type body. The name

Sulcorebutia was coined by Backeberg in 1951, and the genus is based on *S. steinbachii.*

Sulcorebutias are found in the dry valleys of the eastern side of the Bolivian Andes. They grow at altitudes of around 1,800–3,600 m. (6,000–12,000 ft.) and are subjected to frost during the Bolivian winter (July and August).

Most of the sulcorebutias offered for sale are grafted plants. Although they grow and flower well, and form off-sets, there is always the danger of the graft rotting. Reports about re-rooting sulcorebutias suggest that they can often be difficult, although one experienced grower has suggested that these plants re-root slowly but successfully if the cut surface is kept as small as possible, off-sets with narrow 'necks' rooting easily.

On their own roots, sulcorebutias grow without difficulty, if kept in a light position. The flower buds begin to form in the late winter to early spring. After flowering, sulcorebutias, like many South American cacti, have a summer resting period, and start into growth once again in the early autumn.

Sulcorebutias appear to be self-sterile, but hybrids have been formed with *Gymnocalycium, Weingartia* and *Chamaecereus.* At present there is no record of any hybrids with *Rebutia.* At least 25 species of sulcorebutias have been named—an extravagant case of over-splitting. The genus is highly polymorphic and it is difficult to say how many species and varieties are justified.

S. glomerispina is a clustering plant with heads about 5 cm. (2 in.) across. The body is a bluish-green colour and almost covered with brownish spines. These fade to a greyish colour with age. The magenta flowers are about 2 cm. ($\frac{3}{4}$ in.) across.

S. kruegeri has cylindrical heads, and is said to sprout into large clumps, but our own plant has shown no signs of off-sets. The dark green stem is covered with fine spreading pale spines. The flowers are yellow to orange.

S. lepida is a dark green plant with a globular stem up to 3 cm. ($1\frac{1}{4}$ in.) across. It does not form off-sets freely. The spine colour appears to grade through golden-yellow to black: the flowers are carmine-red.

S. steinbachii is a globular, freely-clustering plant with blackish spines. The flower is scarlet.

S. tiraquensis is a large globular plant, about 12 cm. ($4\frac{3}{4}$ in.) across and 5 cm. (2 in.) high. The spines on the new growth are yellow, darkening to various shades of brown or black with age. The flowers are violet.

S. tunariensis is a clustering plant with globular heads, about 2 cm. ($\frac{3}{4}$ in.) across. The spines are yellow when young, turning brown with age; the flowers yellow at the base, and dark red above, and the outside of the petals is purplish-orange.

S. verticillacantha is dark green and spreading, with individual heads about 3 cm. ($1\frac{1}{4}$ in.) across. The spines are brown, later becoming grey. The flowers are light violet to vermilion; if the latter, the petals are often orange towards the base.

Weingartia

Weingartia are very closely related to *Gymnocalycium*; the genus was created in 1933 by Backeberg to accommodate *Weingartia fidaiana* (the type species) and *W. neumanniana*. The species with which most collectors are familiar, *W. cumingii*, was not added to the genus until 1935. There are probably about 10 species. The plants are shortly-cylindrical when mature, the prominent tubercles having large areoles, bearing straight yellow or black spines. The flowers are carried just below the crown and are usually yellow or orange, but occasionally reddish. Unlike gymnocalyciums, the flower tubes are not completely naked. Most of the weingartias come from the Bolivian Andes and are hardy if kept completely dry during the winter.

W. ambigua reaches a height of about 7·5 cm. (3 in.) and has a dull green epidermis with short yellow spines. The flowers of this plant are rather unusual in being of a purple colour, about 2·5 cm. (1 in.) across.

W. cumingii is a very beautiful plant with a bright green epidermis and golden spines, which are not more than 1·25 cm. ($\frac{1}{2}$ in.) long. The flowers are yellow with a red throat.

W. fidaiana is a grey-green plant, about 5 cm. (2 in.) across and with yellow spines, later turning black. It clusters with age. One of its characteristics is a large turnip-like root joined to the body by a narrow neck. The flowers are bright yellow.

W. neumanniana is another grey plant with a swollen root stock. This species has fewer spines than most of the genus; they are yellow, darkening with age and up to about 2·5 to 4 cm. (1 to 1½ in.) long. The flowers are orange-yellow and about 4 cm. (1½ in.) across.

W. westii has a diameter of about 7·5 cm. (3 in.) and eventually reaches a height of about 20 cm. (8 in.). It clusters with age. The stem is dark green with white spines, and is connected by a narrow neck to a large tap-root. The rather small flowers are golden-yellow.

Wigginsia

For many years these plants were known as *Malacocarpus*, but it was discovered that this name had been given earlier to a genus of *Zygophyllaceae* (not cacti). So Porter, in 1964, renamed *Malacocarpus* after a Californian expert on cacti, called Wiggins. Other botanists unite the genus with *Notocactus*.

Wigginsia are found mainly in Uruguay and Argentina. They are amongst the easiest of the cacti to grow and flower and are easily raised from seed. In our experience they are hardy; if dried off in the autumn they should survive a relatively mild winter without heat.

In appearance wigginsias are globular cacti with a woolly crown. The yellow flowers are formed in this wool and are later followed by seed-pods. The flowers are about 5 cm. (2 in.) across. Like many of the notocacti, to which they are closely related, wigginsia flowers have purplish-red lobes to the stigmas.

About 12 species of wigginsias have been described; they all tend to look somewhat alike, as there is little diversity of form or flower colour amongst these plants.

W. corynodes is a globular plant which, with age, forms a dark green cylindrical stem 20 cm. (8 in.) high and 10 cm. (4 in.) across. There are 13–16 ribs and the areoles have 7–12 radials, with one central. These yellow spines are about 2 cm. (¾ in.) long. The yellow flowers yield dark red berries.

W. erinaceus is a dark green globular plant, about 15 cm. (6 in.) across, with 15–20 ribs. There are 6–8 radial spines and one central, about 2 cm. (1¾ in.) long and dark brown in colour.

W. pauciareolatus is again globular, about 12 cm. (4¾ in.) in diameter. There are 15–21 ribs and 4 spines to each areole.

W. sellowii is globular and dark green, up to 15 cm. (6 in.) across, with 16–18 ribs. The areoles carry 5–7 radial spines and one central; they are about 2 cm. ($\frac{3}{4}$ in.) long and yellow in colour. The yellow flowers are followed by pink berries.

NINE

Rare Cacti

Just what constitutes a rare cactus is to some extent a matter of opinion. There are mammillarias which are rarer than ariocarpus, but it would be confusing to discuss them separately from the rest of their genus. So we are including in this chapter only plants where the whole genus is uncommon. Since many of the genera are monotypic, we have not had to worry too much about their common relatives. The following cacti are plants which we ourselves consider as being particularly choice, plants that we would like to see sitting in our own greenhouses (some are already there), if only we could get hold of them. Or, in some cases, if we could afford them.

These cacti are rare in cultivation because they are slow-growing plants which cannot be 'mass produced' in nurseries. They can be grown from seed with patience, but their slow rate of growth makes them a poor commercial proposition. However, a plant raised from seed is invariably a better-looking specimen than an old, imported one. To obtain many of these cacti, it is necessary to buy from a nursery dealing in imported plants. By 'imported plants', we mean cacti that have been wrenched from their native deserts.

Before describing our rare cacti in detail, a few words should be said about imported specimens in general. We have found that buying these cacti can be a chancy business. Sometimes a plant will root easily, others may have been so ill-used in their travels that nothing short of a miracle could do anything for them. Imported cacti are very rarely sold with living roots, and are invariably expensive. So one needs to think carefully before reaching for the cheque book.

Rare Cacti

There is a great deal of controversy about whether one is morally justified in buying rare cacti. In the past, unscrupulous collectors have denuded whole valleys of rarities. Many of these plants died *en route*, and in any case, a single specimen in a greenhouse is for all practical purposes sterile. A few cacti are self-fertile, but these seem to be in the minority. Fortunately governments of central and South America have realised that cacti are a valuable part of their countries' heritage and now control the export of these plants. Most of the really choice cacti are native to Mexico. It is unlikely that plants such as ariocarpus will ever be common in cultivation.

Many of our own rarities have been obtained from the International Succulent Institute of America, whilst others have been bought as seedlings or grown from seed. In those countries where grafting has been perfected, many rare plants are propagated by this method. The top of the scion is cut off, leaving the base on the stock. This base frequently sends out shoots and these, together with the decapitated head, are re-grafted. Using this technique, a single cactus can give rise to large numbers of progeny in a comparatively short time.

Large numbers of the succulent *Lithops optica* forma *rubra* were raised in Germany and replanted in South Africa. Perhaps one day cacti from greenhouses will be used to re-stock their native countries. For the plant collector is not the only enemy of the cactus; there are floods and road building, not to mention the farmer's plough. The plant collector, in fact, in many instances is the cactus' best friend.

Ariocarpus

The name *Ariocarpus* first saw the light of day in 1838 when Dr J. Scheidweiler bestowed it on *Ariocarpus retusus*. Berger split off *A. fissuratus*, *A. fissuratus* var. *lloydii*, and *A. kotschubey-anus* into the genus *Roseocactus*. This last genus is seldom encountered, and Anderson considers that there is insufficient difference between *Roseocactus* and *Ariocarpus* to justify keeping *Roseocactus* as a separate genus. There are six species of *Ariocarpus*, and a number of varieties.

Ariocarpus have a thickened tap-root and a flattened top, with large triangular tubercles. These are almost leaf-like in the sub-genus *Ariocarpus*, but have flat tips in the subgenus *Roseocactus*, together with a thickened, wrinkled skin. The outer tubercles die off with age, and gradually a trunk is formed, with a pattern of old leaf-scars. The flowers are carried at the centre of the plant, usually in the late autumn. Ariocarpus contain alkaloids, but large concentrations are only found in healthy, actively growing plants.

With the exception of *A. fissuratus* and its varieties, these cacti are exclusively Mexican, being found in the Chihuahuan desert. This desert is characterised by the lack of winter rains. The wet period is from July to September, when the rain is often torrential, giving an annual amount of between 25 and 62 cm. (10 and 25 in.).

Many of the ariocarpus that we have seen in cultivation look like fossils. In fact, some of them were undoubtedly dead. But, as their fond owners probably never expected ariocarpus to grow anyway, they were doubtless unaware of this fact. A healthy ariocarpus sends out four or five new tubercles a year, and the centre of the plant should be green, with creamy new wool. The reason for the 'mummies' in so many greenhouses is incorrect cultivation; the owners of these plants have been afraid to water them.

Ariocarpus must be grown in an open compost. We use half grit and half commercial potting compost, to which a pinch of bonemeal has been added. We water freely between April and October; surplus water soon drains off. We also repot annually, for three reasons. Firstly, the food supply of a very open compost is soon exhausted. Secondly, to make sure the roots are healthy and free from mealy bug. Thirdly, ariocarpus swell at the neck; on one occasion *A. trigonus* split its pot and on two other occasions we have had to break the pot to release *A. fissuratus*; a nerve-racking process.

If you water freely and give your ariocarpus new compost annually, it will flourish. One of us was fortunate enough to buy a young *A. furfuraceus* consisting of 4 tubercles. Ten years later this plant has over 40 tubercles and fills a 10-cm. (4-in.) pot. Young plants grow rapidly at first, and then slow down as they reach their maximum size; growing-on young specimens of these plants is quite a practical proposition. Although almost all of the growth of this *A. furfuraceus* was made in our greenhouse, it differs from imported specimens we have seen in only one respect. It is perfect, no scars or battered tubercles.

A. fissuratus is popularly known as the Living Rock, from its resemblance to a chunk of stone. It has been known since 1839, and is found in Mexico and as far north as Texas. A mature specimen is about 15 cm. (6 in.) across and greyish in colour; each tubercle has 3 furrows. The flowers are pink.

A. fissuratus var. *lloydii* is found further south in regions of higher rainfall. The tubercles have only a slight furrow. Since this variety has a more stable water supply, it does not need the wrinkles which allow its close relative to expand and contract in relation to the water content.

A. kotschubeyanus is undoubtedly the easiest of the ariocarpus to flower. The purple flowers appear unfailingly for us each autumn. It is also the ariocarpus most often seen in this country. This species is little more than 5 cm. (2 in.) across, with a flat top and small tubercles. It is clump-forming, but we suspect that the dealers must split up the clumps before selling the plants, as all the specimens we have seen have been single-headed.

A. kotschubeyanus var. *macdowellii* is rather a controversial plant. In appearance it is a miniature version of the above, being less than an inch across, and specimens of this size will flower. Some botanists have considered that *A. macdowellii* is merely an immature form of *A. kotschubeyanus*. We think this is most unlikely; specimens which we have had for years are no larger than when we bought them. Curt Backeberg and the International Succulent Institute consider it a true variety of *A. kotschubeyanus*, and we favour this school of thought. Plants from higher altitudes or drier regions are often smaller than those from more favourable habitats.

A. agavoides is the most recently discovered of the ariocarpus, and with this plant we leave the species with flat tubercles for those with triangular, leaf-like ones. This plant was discovered in 1941 by a Mexican engineer, Castaneda, who named it *Neogomesia agavoides*. It was united with the *Ariocarpus* by E. F. Anderson. After the first few specimens appeared in cultivation,

151

the plant disappeared. Fortunately, the location where the cactus grows was rediscovered and specimens were collected.

This ariocarpus is about 8 cm. (3 in.) across and looks like a miniature agave. The tubercles are ribbed and collect all the particles of dust and sand that are blown about. This is perfect camouflage and explains how *A. agavoides* remained undiscovered for so long. The flowers are large and rose-coloured with a tube 5 cm. (2 in.) long. It flowers in December and some growers suggest keeping this cactus at 10 °C (50 °F) and watering until then.

A. furfuraceus, although sometimes listed, is considered by Anderson to be a variety of *A. retusus*.

A. retusus makes a rosette of triangular green tubercles. We have found it easy to grow; it eventually reaches about 10 cm. (4 in.) across. The flowers are pinkish-white.

A. scapharostrus is not often seen in collections. It is not a beautiful plant, but has the sort of fascination sometimes possessed by the truly ugly. One of us has a young specimen which is very slowly sending up black-green tubercles from the centre. It does not grow with the vigour of a young *A. furfuraceus*. The outer tubercles gradually turn brown and die off; when they are at a half-way stage they have a soft, limp feeling which is at first very worrying. The valuable plant appears to be rotting! But it is only the old tubercles fading away, a perfectly natural process. The tubercles are triangular and upright, whereas those of the preceding plants lean outwards. The ultimate size of *A. scapharostrus* is said to be 10 cm. (4 in.) across. At the present rate of growth of ours we are willing to believe almost anything about the ages of large specimens. The flowers are purple. The natural habitat of this cactus is in very barren ground where it toasts under the Mexican sun; it should be watered with more caution than other species of this genus. Anderson considers this to be the rarest ariocarpus, and that it may prove on further investigation to be a variety of *A. trigonus*.

A. trigonus, the last of the ariocarpus, is also the largest. Specimens growing near streams are reported to be up to 45 cm. (18 in.) across, but the largest plant we have seen in cultivation was about 12 cm. (5 in.). *A. trigonus* clusters, but all the specimens we have met with have been solitary, or the clump has been split before the plants were offered for sale. This plant has long, upright tubercles; it has the shape of the crowns worn by fairy-tale princesses. The flowers are yellow.

Aztekium

Aztekium ritteri is not often offered for sale and old specimens are difficult to re-establish. We had two plants completely mummify before we were lucky enough to get hold of a seedling which rooted without trouble. This cactus was discovered in 1928 by Boedeker. It is found in Mexico, often growing on almost inaccessible cliffs. The ribs of the plant are criss-crossed with furrows which make it look like an Aztec carving. A mature specimen may be as much as 5 cm. (2 in.) across and many of them cluster. The plant body is flattened and almost circular; the new growth is green, fading off to a fawn colour. There are weak spines on the young areoles, but these break off and the base of the plant is naked. The pale pink flowers are found in the wool on top of the plant and last for several days. Unlike many cactus flowers, they are early risers and may well be open before breakfast.

There is only one species.

Blossfeldia

Blossfeldia liliputana is the smallest cactus yet discovered, a mature head being about 2 cm. ($\frac{3}{4}$ in.) across and 5 mm. ($\frac{1}{4}$ in.) high. Fortunately the plant clusters freely; a solitary one might get overlooked. Blossfeldias are grey in colour, spineless, and the areoles are arranged in spirals. They flower in the spring, the colour varying from cream to yellow. The flowers are self-fertile and the seeds germinate easily, but the seedlings are difficult to raise without grafting. Most specimens which appear on the market are grafted, but there is nothing to stop you from removing an off-set and trying it on its own roots, if you consider that the grafted specimens look too plump and lush. These plants are found in northern Argentina at an altitude of 1,900 m. (6,000 ft.) and are happiest under temperate conditions. One grower and importer we know finds that *B. liliputana* grows during the spring and then becomes dormant during the hottest part of the summer. It begins to grow again during the autumn and continues into early winter. He suggests a minimum winter temperature of 7 °C (45 °F) and partial shading in the summer.

Backeberg describes a second species, *B. campaniflora*. This has yellow flowers. At least two other 'species' are sometimes listed in catalogues, *B. minima* and *B. cyathiformis*. In the recently published catalogue of the Zürich collection, these are all reduced to varieties of *B. liliputana*.

Cochemiea

There are five species of *Cochemiea, C. halei, C. maritima, C. pondii, C. poselgeri* and *C. setispina*. The only species likely to be met in cultivation is *C. poselgeri*. This is also the easiest to grow, but since *C. halei* is said to be almost impossible to cultivate, it can be seen that *C. poselgeri* should be approached with caution.

Like many other cacti that are difficult in cultivation, cochemieas are native to Baja California and its adjacent islands. Here the summer temperature reaches 53° C (120 °F) in the shade and there may be no rain for years. It is not easy to believe that the *C. poselgeri* described by plant collectors and explorers is the same plant that one sees in this country. The specimens that we have seen have been about 5 cm. (2 in.) high and usually grafted. One of us owned a small specimen on its own roots but it departed for a happier climate long ago.

In their native land cochemieas are found growing in sandy, gravelly soils, and sometimes even pendent from rocks. *C. poselgeri* is a much-branched plant with stems which can reach a length of 2 m. (6 ft.). The prominent tubercles are spirally arranged and the scarlet flowers form a ring around the top of the stem. They are narrowly tubular and about 4 cm. (1½ in.) long. Some writers have described the flowers of cochemieas as being reminiscent of an aporocactus or schlumbergera.

Rare Cacti

Epithelantha

Epithelantha are amongst the easiest of the rarities to obtain. Since they cluster freely, it is not difficult to propagate these plants on a commercial scale.

At the present moment, there seems to be some confusion as to the numbers of species and varieties in this genus. *E. micromeris* and *E. m.* var. *greggii* are definitely recognised. Varieties such as *tuberosa*, *fungifera*, *longicaulis* and *unguispina* are mentioned in catalogues, but many authorities consider these as geographical variations of *E. micromeris*. The Zürich collection considers only two species, *E. micromeris* and its varieties, and *E. pachyriza*.

E. micromeris is found growing on limestone hills in Texas and northern Mexico. The stems of this cactus are globular and covered with dense white spines. From a distance they look rather like table-tennis balls. Usually *E. micromeris* forms clumps; very old specimens have over a hundred heads. The pinkish-white flowers are carried on top of the plant; these are followed by attractive red berries.

E. micromeris var. *greggii* is larger than the above plant. It has longer tubercles and a well-developed central spine. These epithelanthas have two things in common; they are very slow-growing and need watering carefully.

Encephalocarpus

Encephalocarpus strobiliformis is one of the easiest of the Mexican imports to grow. A porous soil and plenty of water in summer and the plant will thrive. It is also very free-flowering, growing a succession of bright purple blooms during the summer. It is an interesting fact that a number of these rare Mexican cacti, including *E. strobiliformis*, open their flowers in dull, cloudy weather. In very poor summers we have seen the buds on lobivias and echinopsis dry up, but plants such as encephalocarpus, pelecyphoras and toumeyas, which come from regions of fierce sunlight, bloom as if nothing had gone wrong with the weather.

Encephalocarpus is considered by a number of botanists to be closely related to *Ariocarpus*. There is only one species in the genus. In appearance, *E. strobiliformis* looks like a fawn-coloured pine cone, the stem being covered with tiny overlapping scales. Some writers describe the plant as globular. When first bought our plant was spherical, but it has long since outgrown this shape and is now cylindrical. The top of the plant is covered in white wool from which the buds protrude. Some specimens form clumps; one of us owns a plant which was obviously one head of a group, since the body is set at an angle to the root, which makes it very difficult to pot up. If the stem is straight the root is at an awkward angle; for the sake of beauty we keep the stem upright and give the roots a slightly larger pot than would be necessary if we did not tilt them.

Leuchtenbergia

L. principis has been known in cultivation for a long time; it received its name from a botanist, Hooker, in 1848. The rather curious name comes from Eugène de Beauharnais, Prince of Leuchtenberg, who was a great patron of horticulture.

This genus is monotypic, the one and only species is found in central and northern Mexico. It is a strange-looking cactus, which at first glance could easily be mistaken for an agave. It has a thickened root with a trunk-like stem on top of which are slender grey tubercles about 12 cm. (5 in.) long. Sometimes leuchtenbergias are double-headed; we have had quite small seedlings branch dichotomously. The great beauty of this plant is in its lemon-coloured flowers which are about 8 cm. (3 in.) long and very sweetly scented.

Leuchtenbergias are easily raised from seed and the little seedlings are miniature versions of the adult.

Lophophora

These are probably the easiest of the 'rare cacti' to grow from seed, and since the plants are self-fertile, there is no problem about obtaining seed. A seedling *Lophophora* will flower when about 2·5 cm. (1 in.) across; this is usually at about five or six years of age. The blooms are produced continuously throughout the summer.

Lophophoras are found in Mexico and southern Texas and

have been known since the 16th century, when early explorers thought they were fungi. They were first encountered as 'mescal buttons', being dried slices threaded on cords and sold in the Mexican markets. Since 'mescal' is the word for fungus, the mistake was natural. Following their recognition as cacti, they travelled through several genera before Coulter created the genus *Lophophora* in 1894. One of the early names, *Anhalonium*, is still occasionally met in older writings.

These plants are famous, or perhaps infamous for containing, among other alkaloids, mescalin. This is said to increase colour perception, if it does not make one too disgustingly sick to be aware of anything! To the Mexican Indians, the lophophora, or Peyotl, still is a sacred plant, playing an important part in ceremonies designed to placate the gods and ensure good harvests. However, the Indians do not just sit around chewing the dried plant in a mass orgy. They go through a series of fasts and taboos that would discourage even the most ardent seeker after sensations.

L. williamsii is the species most frequently seen. A mature specimen is about 8 cm. (3 in.) across and will have a few off-sets. These can be removed and re-rooted, but the parent plant is scarred in the process. Sometimes a grafted lophophora is seen that has gone 'berserk' and produced dozens of small heads. These can be gouged off, but are difficult to root; however, they re-graft very easily.

The plant has a large tap-root and a low domed head, divided into clear cut ribs. The areoles are spineless but have small tufts of wool. Pink flowers are carried in the wool on top of the plant, the body of which is of a silvery-grey colour. A fascinating cristate form is sometimes seen.

L. lewenii was once considered to be a variety of *L. williamsii*, but is now classed as a separate species. Buxbaum states that it contains a different alkaloid from the other two species. This does not greatly help the collector, who will hardly be able to analyse the plant before paying for it. Borg describes it as being larger than *L. williamsii*, with more ribs. Our own plant is a young seedling and is much too immature for us to decide how it will end up. But although less than 2 cm. ($\frac{3}{4}$ in.) across, it has a tiny off-set.

L. ziegleri; here one is on much firmer ground. This has pale yellow or whitish flowers and the head is not neatly divided into regular ribs as in the other two species, but rather into lightly marked grooves. It also forms off-sets.

Mamillopsis

There are two species of *Mamillopsis*, although they are some-times considered as varieties of only one. These cacti are found high up in the mountains of Mexico, where they pass the winter under the snow. We know of collectors who grow them without heat in this country, but if so they must be kept bone dry in winter.

M. senilis is the species most often seen. In appearance it is like a fluffy white ball, being completely covered in silvery-white spines about 1 cm. (⅜ in.) long. It is probably one of the most beautiful cacti to come out of Mexico. A mature specimen will cluster, the heads eventually reaching about 8 cm. (3 in.) across. The red flowers are borne on top of the plant; they are over 5 cm. (2 in.) long and almost as much across. Seed is available and home-raised seedlings are less prone to rot than imported plants. In any case, a very open soil and a dry winter rest are particularly important.

M. diguetii, sometimes considered a variety of *M. senilis,* has orange flowers, smaller than those of the latter, but the spines are stronger. It is very much rarer.

Obregonia

Obregonia denegrii is a Mexican cactus discovered by Fric in 1925, and is the only species in the genus. The plants are found growing on hillsides in the shade of small bushes and boulders. But it must be emphasised that the Mexican sun is not the English sun; the problem in this country is to give your *O. denegrii* sufficient sunlight. It is one of the rare cacti that can be raised from seed without too much difficulty, and it will flower in a reasonable time. In appearance, *O. denegrii* is almost globular, with white wool on top. The stem is covered with leaf-like tubercles which are almost brown in colour. The plant will eventually reach a diameter of about 12 cm. (5 in.), and some specimens form clumps. Obregonias flower when about 5–8 cm. (2–3 in.) across, the blooms being produced on and off during the summer from the wool at the top of the plant. The petals are very narrow and of a striking shining white.

The cultivation of these cacti is easy, provided they are given a porous soil. If watered freely during summer, they grow vigorously.

Pediocactus

P. simpsonii is found on the Pacific side of the United States, where it covers the region from Washington down to New Mexico, and also in Colorado. It is surprising that a plant which covers such a large area and has been known since 1846 should be so rarely seen in cultivation. Backeberg suggests that this is due to the difficulty of reproducing its natural conditions in most greenhouses. *P. simpsonii* has a very short growing period, most of its life is spent tucked away under a layer of snow in its native mountainous regions.

Pediocactus simpsonii is about 15 cm. (6 in.) in diameter and is covered with tubercles which are arranged on spiral ribs. The areoles are well equipped with numerous spines about 2.5 cm. (1 in.) long. The flowers are pink.

There appear to be several varieties of *P. simpsonii* but probably only one species. The varieties are *minor, robustior* and *caespitosus*. This last variety as described by Backeberg can have as many as 50 heads, but much smaller than those of the type plant. *Pilacanthus paradinei* is now included in the genus *Pediocactus*. Old specimens have long, dense, white hairs.

Pelecyphora

The *Pelecyphora* must be among the slowest growing of the cacti. Every year *P. valdeziana* grows a little new white wool on top, but each year it flowers freely, so there must be new areoles somewhere underneath.

'Pelecyphora' means 'hatchet-bearing', and *P. aselliformis* in particular has tubercles with an axe-head form. These Mexican cacti contain alkaloids similar to the lophophoras, and share the vernacular name 'peyote' or 'peyotillo' with this genus. *P. aselliformis* even has a railway station named after it, Hacienda de Peotilla. Pelecyphoras were collected in this area for the treatment of fevers.

P. aselliformis is the species most frequently met. This has pectinate or comb-like white spines which give the tubercles a resemblance to a woodlouse, hence the name. The plant body is cylindrical and covered with white spines, but the base of the stem becomes corky with age. Sometimes it is possible to buy clumps, but usually these are split up before sale. The violet flowers are produced freely during the summer and arise from the top of the plant.

P. pseudopectinata is the most beautiful of the pelecyphoras and slightly faster growing than the other two species. The numerous fine spines cover the body completely, giving the impression of a snow-white plant. The pale pink flowers open in late winter.

P. valdenziana is the smallest member of this genus, and it has had a somewhat chequered career; at one time it was considered to be a thelocactus. It is a solitary plant with small tubercles covered in short white spines, arranged in the typical comb-like formation. The violet flowers appear in late winter. Our own specimen has flowered for years, when suddenly one year it set seed. There was no other cactus in bloom at the time. The seed germinated well, but the seedlings are incredibly slow-growing. It has never set seed since.

All these plants need a particularly open compost. We water the two winter-flowering specimens on sunny days once the flower buds are well developed.

Porfiria

P. schwartzii is a small cactus closely related to *Mammillaria*, and is the only representative of the genus. This little Mexican has a turnip-like root and a globular stem scarcely more than 2·5 cm. (1 in.) high. The pale pink flowers are over 2·5 cm.

(1 in.) across, and the whitish spines are borne on prominent tubercles. *P. schwartzii* is a very slow-growing plant, and should be watered with great caution; overwet root conditions are likely to cause rot very easily. An open compost is essential.

Sclerocactus

Sclerocactus are found in the southern part of the United States, New Mexico, Colorado, Nevada and Arizona. There are four species that one is likely to come across; *Sclerocactus whipplei*, *S. polyancistrus*, *S. intermedius*, and *S. alba. S. whipplei* itself tends to vary considerably, depending on its habitat and it is difficult to say where one species ends and the next begins. Doubtless one day this problem will be sorted out.

The cultivation of sclerocacti is not easy. They are found at altitudes as high as 1,900 m. (6,000 ft.) and are perfectly hardy in a dry atmosphere. They come from a very dry region where the soil is stony and open. To succeed with these plants in cultivation they need a cold, dry winter, a very open compost, and watering with great caution.

S. whipplei is the species most likely to be met. It has prominent warty ribs with stout spines. Some specimens cluster freely, whilst others remain solitary. The size of the heads is variable; specimens have been described with stems varying from 5–30 cm. (2–12 in.). Likewise the flower colour seems to vary from one habitat to another. White, pale pink, and purple have been recorded.

Solisia

S. pectinata is one of the cacti about which the botanists are still undecided. In many ways it superficially resembles the pelecyphoras and was included in that genus by Stein in 1885. It has the hatchet-shaped tubercles and beautiful close white spines of these cacti. But it has also certain affinities to the mammillarias; milky sap, and the pink flowers arise from the sides of the plant. Buxbaum includes *Solisia* among the subgenera of his genus *Mammillaria*. Until the experts make up their minds, there is a lot to be said for leaving this plant under *Solisia*, where it was placed by Britton and Rose.

Solisia pectinata is found in Mexico, but even in its native land it is scarce. It makes a stem 5–8 cm. (2–3 in.) high. It is not easy to flower in cultivation. We have had our plant several years and, although it grows well, it has had no flowers. On the same shelf, the pelycyphoras bloom profusely.

Strombocactus

At one time the genus *Strombocactus* contained a number of species, but it is now reduced to one, *S. disciformis*. The other species have been removed to the genus *Toumeya*.

S. disciformis gets its specific name from the Greek word *diskos*. Certainly we have seen thin, disc-like plants; our own are plump and almost hemispherical. The purist might say they are over-lush, but they have been flowering from February to October for the last 10 years, so we are not worrying. The flowers are pale cream. The young tubercles are bright green, turning greyish with age. There is a great deal of white wool on top of the plant from which the flower buds emerge. The new areoles carry spines which fall off with age. This plant is found in Mexico, whole colonies appearing on baking hot hillsides. They are difficult to find when not in flower since they become powdered with dust and sand which blends them into the hillside. Strombo-cacti are easy to grow and flower; even in the greyest of summers there is a profusion of creamy blooms.

Toumeya

This is rather a patchwork genus. It is made up of plants which were once known as *Strombocactus*, *Turbinicarpus*, *Navajoa*, and *Toumeya papyracantha*.

Toumeyas are small, globular cacti with spiral ribs. The flowers are carried on the top of the plant. New discoveries are being made in this group of plants, but specimens are not readily available. Species which are occasionally offered are *T. pseudo-macrothele*, *T. lophophoroides* and *T. schmiedickeana*.

Rare Cacti

Uebelmannia

This is a genus of cacti which at the moment of writing is rare in collections, although some are available if you can afford them.

Uebelmannia come from the mountains of Brazil and some species have been discovered as recently as 1966. There are at least three species. *U. gummifera, U. pectinifera,* and *U. buiningii.* These last two species are solitary plants, with a dark brown epidermis and yellow flowers. *U. pectinifera* is found growing in between rocks amongst bromeliads. This part of the world has heavy rainfall during the summer. The lower part of *U. pectinifera* is often covered with lichens.

Utahia

U. sileri is occasionally offered for sale, but it is not an easy plant to re-establish. We tried our hands with an imported, rootless plant, but we never got it away. These cacti come from Utah. They are most noted for their stout black and white spines which cover the plant. The flowers are yellow.

TEN

Epiphytes and other Large-flowered Cacti

THE EPIPHYTES

Although most cacti are native to the desert regions, as we have mentioned earlier, there are also jungle types, the epiphytic cacti. An epiphyte is a plant growing on another plant, usually a tree, but this is used only as a support, no nourishment being obtained from it, as in the case of a parasite. Other well-known examples of epiphytic plants are many bromeliads and orchids. These plants are usually to be found growing in pockets of leaf debris in the forks of tree branches. Because they have access to only small amounts of soil, some ability to conserve water or collect moisture from the usually damp atmosphere is necessary. Different types of epiphytes have evolved various means of doing this; the cacti naturally having succulent stems, although these are less fleshy than the more typical desert types.

The epiphytic cacti are found in the forests of tropical America. Whereas the desert cacti tend to be globular, or columnar and ribbed, the jungle cacti usually consist of long trailing or pendulious green stems. These may be cylindrical or flat; some are jointed, whilst others are unbranched, continuous stems several metres in length. Some of these stems have small spines, some are spineless; the ferocious armour of many of the more typical cacti is absent. Aerial roots are present in some of the epiphytes to enable them to absorb the moisture in the air more effectively and cling to supports. Many have large, showy flowers, of which we shall have more to say in the appropriate sections. The rather dark, moist forest conditions under which the epiphytes live give

164

us important clues for their successful cultivation. We shall describe a number of these cacti, but as the general requirements of the various genera are much the same, we shall group them together for the purpose of cultivation.

Epiphytes have been mentioned briefly in the chapter on cultivation, but it is appropriate to go into the matter a little more fully here. As they grow in comparatively small pockets of leaf-mould, they tend not to have large root systems and flower better if not overpotted. Leafmould is a good source of plant nutrient, so a rich soil is needed. However, for those not wishing to make up their own composts, one of the prepared peat composts is quite suitable.

These natural soil pockets are loose, the roots of the plants having free access to moist air, so our soil should be open, with good drainage, and not allowed to become compressed. Again, because of the moist growing conditions, these cacti dislike drying out, and regular watering is essential, particularly in hot weather. Although a greenhouse of 'desert' cacti is not really the best place in which to grow epiphytes, like most cacti, they are quite accommodating, and will grow satisfactorily under these conditions, provided that they are given an occasional spray with water. The natural pockets of leafmould are rather acid, and these cacti particularly dislike an alkaline soil; if possible very hard water should not be given to them. If rain water is not available, the hard water can be acidulated by adding a few drops of nitric or phosphoric acid to each gallon of water, although in most cases ordinary tap water can be given without apparent harm.

Epiphytes being native to woodland regions grow at their best in filtered sun or semi-shade. Most of them can stand low winter temperatures as well as other cacti, a minimum of 5 °C (41 °F) being sufficient. We shall mention the exceptions.

Epiphyllum

We shall deal first with the *Epiphyllum*, out of strict alphabetical order, since plants popularly covered by this name are by far the best-known amongst the epiphytes. However, under this heading, we must consider two different types of cactus, the true *Epiphyllum* and the cultivated garden hybrids. The former are as rare in cultivation as the latter are common.

The name epiphyllum means literally 'upon the leaf', referring to the position of the flowers, although the so-called 'leaves' are in fact true stems. The old name, 'Phyllocactus', or 'leaf cactus' is equally misleading. In appearance, epiphyllums consist of elongated stems a metre (39 in.) or more in length, either flat or angled, often with small spines arising from the areoles, which are carried along the edges of the stems.

The 'wild' species epiphyllums are not often found in cultivation. They are large plants, rather tender, and needing a higher winter temperature than most cacti, about 10 °C (50° F). The large flowers are white and mostly nocturnal. Three of these species plants that the reader may come across are:

E. anguliger, from south Mexico, has beautiful deeply-cut branches. The white flowers are of a medium size, about 15 cm. (6 in.) long. They are lemon-scented and produced in the autumn.

E. crenatum comes from Honduras and Guatemala, and is one of the species much used in raising hybrids. The branches are stiff and thin at the edges. The erect plant reaches a height of about 1 m. (39 in.) and the branches may be 60 cm. (2 ft.) long and 6 cm. ($2\frac{1}{4}$ in.) broad. The flowers are up to 20 cm. (8 in.) across and white.

E. oxypetalum (or *E. latifrons*) from Mexico to Brazil, has white, scented flowers 12 cm. ($4\frac{3}{4}$ in.) broad. The long stems are almost cylindrical. The flowers open at night and this is one of the so-called 'Queen of the Night' cacti.

The hybrid epiphyllums are in a somewhat different class, and it is these which are so popular amongst many flower lovers, who would probably not consider growing 'cacti'. They are polygenetic hybrids and some may have no true epiphyllum ancestry at all. They have been developed for their greater hardiness than the species and their profusion of large, longer-lasting flowers in a range of colours. It is in their magnificent flowers that their great beauty lies, for out of flower, the long green stems are not particularly interesting. Because of these bright, large blooms, the hybrid epiphyllums are often known as 'Orchid Cacti', although the flowers themselves bear little resemblance to those of orchids in shape.

The first of these hybrid cacti were developed over 100 years ago in Europe from two imported cacti, *Nopalxochia phyllan-thoides*, an epiphyte, and *Heliocereus speciosus*, which is not an epiphyte but a terrestrial species. Many fine hybrids were produced and by crossing these in turn with various species *Epiphyllum*, the hundreds of present-day hybrids have been produced. The original hybrids were red-flowered, but today many colours are available; various shades of red and pink to orange, yellow and white. These flowers last for several days, and the buds will open even if the weather should be dull, in contrast to many of the desert cacti. In spite of their non-epiphytic ancestor, the hybrid epiphyllums can be cultivated as already described for epiphytes in general.

There are so many of these hybrids available that it is difficult to pick out just a few, but we have made a selection of those we consider to be amongst the best. Many others are described in the lists of specialist nurseries. These cacti are widely grown in the United States as greenhouse plants, and a society is entirely devoted to them. As they are hybrids they are given cultivar names only: in some cases the ancestors are known and mentioned.

'Ackermannii' is a *Heliocereus* × *Nopalxochia* hybrid, and is correctly called × *Heliochia* 'Ackermannii'. It has a medium, salmon-red flower with white stamens; funnel form, very free flowering, often again in autumn and winter as well as spring.
'Bens Laura', large, flat-opening, pearly flower with numerous chiffon-like petals.
'Bruxelles', large, bright scarlet flower with purple style. Very free flowering and particularly suitable for hanging baskets.
'Cooperi' is a hybrid between *Selinicereus grandiflorus* and *Epiphyllum crenatum*. It correct name is × *Seleniphyllum cooperi* 'Cooperi'. It blooms late in the season. The flower is large and with an open funnel shape. The inner petals are snow-white, and the outer golden-yellow and brown. The flowers open in the evening; they have a strong, lily-like perfume. Instead of arising from the upper parts of the stems, as in most of the hybrids, the flowers are produced from the base of the plant.

'Dante' has blood-red petals, with purple shading inside the open cup form flower. The throat is green, the stamens pale pink and the pistil red.

'Deutsche Kaiserin' is a hybrid of *Nopalxochia phyllanthoides*. It has the medium, pink flowers of this plant, is very free blooming, and ideal for hanging baskets.

'Dr. Werdermann', rich rose-purple in colour, with an orange centre stripe. Extra large flower of an open cup form.

'Eastern Trance', Auger hybrid, 1967. Large broad-petalled flower, rose-pink, deepening to delft rose; good strong growth.

'Eden', large, open cup-shape, fine white bloom with yellow back petals; free flowering.

'Friedrich Werner Beul' has one of the largest flowers, flat with broad petals, outer red, inner crimson-orange, shading to lavender and white edges.

'June Bride' has a medium, funnel-shaped flower, cream and white. Free flowering.

'Kathleen Heatley', a small-growing plant with very large, brilliant, open red flowers, with slight yellow sheen.

'London Glory', one of the many hybrids raised by F. R. McQuown, to which he gave the prefix 'London'. This plant has large red flowers, freely produced in summer. The fruits are large, red and sweet.

'London Sunshine', another 'London' hybrid, of a mimosa yellow, cup and saucer shape, free flowering.

'Midnight' has purple flowers, with pink edges, giving a blue effect. Very large, open cup and saucer bloom. Free flowering.

'Old Vienna' is a good new hybrid with purple and orange blooms and red centre stripe.

'Padre', large, funnel-form pink flowers, strong growth and abundance of flowers. Blooms early, sometimes in winter.

'Phantom', large, open flower with narrow, glowing white inner petals and creamy outer.

'Pride of San Gabriel' has flowers with a wide central stripe over deep purple. They are wide open with ruffled sepals and petals.

'Professor Ebert', fuchsia-red blooms with a flat funnel-form, large and double. The finest of this colour and an excellent grower.

'Purple Dawn' is strong-growing with well-formed red and purple flowers.

'Sunburst', large, wide funnel: burnt salmon with red eye. Extremely heavy flowerer on small plant growth. Sturdy.
'Thalia', large, wide open-funnel-form flowers. Petals salmon-red, magenta shading, with distinct yellow stripe; edge of petals ruffled.
'Truce', a 1964 Auger hybrid. Very large, pure white flower with recurving green back petals. Open cup form.
'Valse Brilliant', a wide open purple flower, smooth pointed petals.
'Wanderlust', a full-petalled, dark pink flower with small cherry throat. Three overlapping tiers of petals, with ruffled edges.
'Wrayi', large cup and saucer form; creamy-white, with yellow back petals, sweetly scented. Another × *Seleniphyllum.*

Having dealt with the epiphyllums and their hybrids, we return to the consideration of the other epiphytes. Many of these cacti, although not extensively grown, are deserving of mention, but we shall only discuss them briefly, leaving more space for those few that are in general cultivation.

Acanthorhipsalis

These are bushy shrubs with flat or 3-angled stems, 2–6 cm. ($\frac{3}{4}$–$2\frac{1}{4}$ in.) broad and up to 40 cm. (16 in.) long, according to the species. The natural habitat is Peru, east Bolivia and north Argentina where the plants mostly grow epiphytically, or on rocks at altitudes from 1,500–2,600 m. (5,000–8,500 ft.). Backeberg lists 5 species; they are very similar to *Rhipsalis,* except for the possession of spines in the areoles.
A. micrantha is the type species, from Peru. The much-branched stems are 2 cm. ($\frac{3}{4}$ in.) broad and up to 20 cm. (8 in.) long. There are 3–10 spines at each areole, up to 1·5 cm. ($\frac{5}{8}$ in.) long. The purple flowers may be up to 2·5 cm. (1 in.) in length.
A. monacantha, from north Argentina, forms a branched bush up to about 1 m. (3 ft.) high, with leaf-like joints. The areoles have yellowish wool, and there are one or two stiff brown spines. The white flowers are about 1 cm. ($\frac{3}{8}$ in.) long.

Chiapasia

C. nelsonii is the only species described. It is a plant very similar to an *Epiphyllum*, with slender stems up to about 1 m. (39 in.) long, at first erect, later hanging. The branches are 10–25 cm. (4–10 in.) long and 3–4 cm. (1¼–1⅝ in.) across and notched. The carmine-red flowers, with curved petals, are carried on the upper parts of the branches; they are 7–8 cm. (about 3 in.) long and sweetly scented. Unfortunately, this plant does not appear to flower readily in cultivation, and is not particularly easy to come by.

Disocactus

These are plants of similar habit of growth to *Epiphyllum*, with cylindrical and flat stems, up to about 30 cm. (1 ft.) long and branching. The flowers are small, diurnal and red in colour. Borg mentions 2 species, *D. biformis* and *D. eichlamii*.

Epiphyllanthus

This genus is now included under *Schlumbergera* by Hunt.

Erythrorhipsalis

Berger created the genus for the plant originally described as *Rhipsalis pilocarpa,* due to slight differences in the flower compared with other *Rhipsalis*. However, these differences are not now considered sufficient to justify a separate genus, and this plant is described under *Rhipsalis*.

Hatiora

Hatiora are closely related to *Rhipsalis*. Most authors recognise about 3 species, but by far the best known is *Hatiora salicornioides* and the others may well be merely varieties of this. In appearance *H. salicornioides* resembles somewhat the Glassworts or *Salicornia*, hence the name (*Salicornia* are succulent plants found on salt marshes and saline ground, and have no relationship with cacti). The plant is spineless, freely branching and with many clavate, or bottle-shaped joints, 1–3 cm. (⅜–1¼ in.) long and

4–7 mm. ($\frac{1}{8}$–$\frac{1}{4}$ in.) thick. An areole is carried on the tip of each branch, and from these arise small greenish-yellow flowers in February. Although small, *en masse*, they are quite attractive. Cuttings root easily and a small bush is quickly formed. These little, unusual-looking cacti are easy to cultivate, requiring the typical epiphyte conditions and, unlike most of the rhipsalis, they can tolerate comparative drought. They should, however, be kept moist during winter, for extreme dryness at the roots can cause shedding of the joints. Large temperature fluctuations and cold draughts should be avoided for the same reason.

Lepismium

Most botanists now consider this genus to be hardly separable from *Rhipsalis*, and it will be found under that heading.

Nopalxochia

N. phyllanthoides is a very epiphyllum-like plant and was one of the original ancestors of the epiphyllum hybrids. It has cylindrical main stems with rather thin flattened branches. The pink flowers are about 5 cm. (2 in.) across and remain open during daytime. They are freely produced, but scentless. This cactus probably originated in Mexico but as it has been in cultivation for so long, the exact native habitat is uncertain. The hybrid 'Deutsche Kaiserin' (described under *Epiphyllum*) was for a long time considered to be a form of *N. phyllanthoides,* but it is now regarded as one of the hybrids between this and *Heliocereus speciosus*. The species *N. ackermannii* is confused in cultivation with its hybrid with *Heliocereus speciosus*, giving the so-called 'Ackermannii hybrid' (see under *Epiphyllum*), which is far more likely to be met.

Pfeiffera

P. ianthothele, from north Argentina, is the species usually seen, although the Zürich collection lists also *P. gracilis* and *P. multigona*. *P. ianthothele* has 3- or 4-angled stems, about 30 cm. (1 ft.) long and 2 cm. ($\frac{3}{4}$ in.) thick, of a pale green colour. Thin, bristly spines are carried by the areoles along the angles. The bell-shaped flowers are small, about 2 cm. ($\frac{3}{4}$ in.) long. This plant is self-fertile, fruits rather like small gooseberries being freely produced. The black seeds are embedded in a mass of pulp. This cactus makes a good subject for a hanging basket.

Rhipsalidopsis

R. gaertneri (Easter Cactus). This plant was formerly known as *Schlumbergera gaertneri*, but has now been transferred to *Rhipsalidopsis,* mainly because of its slightly different flower structure. The plant itself is very similar to the schlumbergera hybrids, consisting of many leaf-like joints with serrated edges and small, bristly spines. The regular scarlet flowers appear later than those of most schlumbergeras, around Easter time, hence the common name. It comes from Brazil.

R. rosea was the original sole species of the genus, which was separated from *Rhipsalis* because of its comparatively large flowers. It is native to the forests of south Brazil. The plant consists of much-branched stems composed of many small joints, flat or angled, about 2 cm. ($\frac{3}{4}$ in.) long. The rose-pink, regular flowers are freely produced in early spring. They are about 2·5 cm. (1 in.) across. This is a most attractive little plant.

As in the case of the Christmas Cactus, to be mentioned later, hybrids of these plants have been produced, and given cultivar names. Examples of these are: 'Paleface', 'Salmon Queen', 'Spring Dazzler', and 'Spring Princess'. The cultivation of these hybrids is very similar to that suggested for the Christmas Cactus. They flower in the spring.

Rhipsalis

The name *Rhipsalis* comes from the Greek word *rhips,* meaning 'wicker-work', and refers to the long, thin, interlacing branches of many of the species. These have a superficial resemblance to mistletoe. Others, however, are more like smaller, slender epiphyllums. They are much-branched plants with cylindrical, angular or flat, leaf-like stems, with many joints. The areoles are distributed along the margins of the angular or flat joints, and scattered around the cylindrical stems. They often carry wool, hair or bristles. The flowers are small but last up to about a week.

Epiphytes and other Large-flowered Cacti

In 1959 Backeberg recognised 60 species, occurring from Florida and the West Indies, through Mexico to Argentina. As mentioned in the chapter 'What is a Cactus?', there are some species of rhipsalis which are unique amongst cacti in apparently having their natural habitat outside the American continent, although it is now believed that they were introduced. In spite of the many species, the non-specialist grower is likely to encounter only a few. The cultural suggestions already mentioned for epiphytes are suitable for rhipsalis, most of which are ideal for hanging baskets. Any readers who grow orchids can grow these cacti in the same way, and with the same compost.

R. anceps, from east Brazil, has flat or 3-angled branches, about 40 cm. (16 in.) long and 1·5 cm. ($\frac{5}{8}$ in.) broad. There are hairs or bristles on the areoles. The flowers, on the side areoles, are violet.

R. cassytha, the type plant of the genus, forms a hanging bush, over 1 m. (39 in.) long, consisting of cylindrical joints without bristles. These joints are 10–20 cm. (4–8 in.) long, and around 3 mm. ($\frac{1}{8}$ in.) thick. The greenish-white flowers are about 5 mm. ($\frac{1}{4}$ in.) long. The plant comes from Florida to south Brazil, and has also been found in tropical Africa and Ceylon.

R. cereuscula is one of the more common rhipsalis in cultivation and more drought resistant than most species. The shoots are up to 40 cm. (16 in.) long, narrow, and branched at the ends. These branches are short and cylindrical with white, hairy spines at the tips. The areoles, scattered over the surface of the stems, carry white bristly spines. The green flowers are borne at the tips of the short branches and are about 1·5 cm. ($\frac{5}{8}$ in.) long. The native habitat is east Brazil to Uruguay and Argentina.

R. cruciforme was originally classified under *Rhipsalis,* and subsequently transferred to a newly created genus, *Lepismium.* The latter, however, is now considered better united once more with *Rhipsalis.* Although several species have been described, they are possibly variations of *R. cruciforme,* itself variable. The long, slender joints are flat or 3-angled and toothed, with bristly spines in the areoles. The greenish flowers are about 1 cm. ($\frac{3}{8}$ in.) long.

R. elliptica is a broad-stemmed species somewhat resembling a schlumbergera. The joints are leaf-like and about 6 cm. ($2\frac{1}{4}$ in.) long and 2·5 cm. (1 in.) across, dark green and slightly notched at the margins. The flowers are less than 1 cm. ($\frac{3}{8}$ in.) long and white. From east and south Brazil.

R. houlletiana is a much-branched plant from east Brazil with tall, erect, cylindrical stems, and two types of joint; very thin, stiff, cylindrical ones, and others flat and leaf-like, about 10 cm. (4 in.) long and 2·5 cm. (1 in.) broad, toothed. The cream flowers are freely produced from the edge areoles and are about 1·5 cm. ($\frac{5}{8}$ in.) long.

R. mesembryanthemoides is a shrubby plant, again with two types of stem, upright, cylindrical ones about 30 cm. (1 ft.) long, and numerous short side branches, about 1 cm. ($\frac{3}{8}$ in.) long and 3 mm. ($\frac{1}{8}$ in.) thick. The brown, slightly woolly areoles carry small spines. Small white flowers are carried at the tips of the short branches. The native habitat is the Rio de Janeiro area of east Brazil.

R. pilocarpa. This was formerly known as *Erythrorhipsalis pilocarpa*, the genus *Erythrorhipsalis* having been created by Berger to contain one *Rhipsalis* species which he thought sufficiently different to warrant a separate genus. However, this plant is not now considered to require separation. *R. pilocarpa* comes from Sao Paulo and Rio de Janeiro, Brazil. The stems are dark green, cylindrical, and up to 40 cm. (16 in.) long, only 3–6 cm. ($\frac{1}{8}$–$\frac{1}{4}$ in.) in diameter. The areoles carry greyish bristles. The scented flowers are borne at the tips of the branches, white or cream in colour and up to 2 cm. ($\frac{3}{4}$ in.) across. They appear in winter, and the fruits are red.

R. warmingiana, also from east Brazil, has flat or angled stems up to 30 cm. (1 ft.) long and 2 cm. ($\frac{3}{4}$ in.) broad. The areoles are woolly, but without spines or bristles. The cream flowers open early in the year and are followed by almost black fruits, which have been likened to blackcurrants.

Schlumbergera

Readers of earlier books will have found the 'Easter Cactus' referred to as *Schlumbergera gaertneri*. Now, however, it is considered to be a *Rhipsalidopsis*, and will be found under that heading. This leaves us with only two species *Schlumbergera,* both rather unlikely to be found in collections, as the situation is complicated by the presence of many hybrids.

S. russelliana comes from Rio de Janeiro, and is the seed parent of the Christmas Cactus, shortly to be described. The flowers are regular with no perianth tube. They are bright carmine and are produced around February. This, and the following plant, is pollinated by humming birds.

S. truncata is the other (pollen) parent of the Christmas Cactus. Several cultivars have been known for a long time. The typical *S. truncata* has carmine zygomorphic flowers and truncated stem segments, with definite 'teeth' at the ends.

There is considerable confusion amongst the many varieties and hybrids of these two cacti and much research has been carried out on their history, notably by W. L. Tjaden. However, the average grower and collector is more likely to be interested in the plants themselves, without being too bothered about giving each a precise name.

This is the most convenient place to deal with the Christmas Cactus, which has for so long been known as *Zygocactus truncatus*. Research into the origins of this old-established plant by Tjaden has shown that it is in fact a hybrid between *Schlumbergera russelliana* and *S. truncata*, to which genus *Zygocactus* is now referred as a synonym. The hybrid in question was raised by William Buckley in the late 1840s, and is now known as *Schlumbergera × buckleyi* cv. 'Buckleyi' (cv. meaning 'cultivar'). The typical 'Buckleyi' hybrid has pink stamens, but a second plant was raised by Buckley with white stamens, and known as 'Rollissonii'. It is a somewhat more spreading plant than the 'Buckleyi' hybrid. Since both these plants exist, together with various intermediate forms and back-crosses, it is convenient to use the name Christmas Cactus for them. The rejected name, *Zygocactus truncatus*, will no doubt be used in gardening books for many years to come.

The typical Christmas Cactus consists of a number of flattened stem segments (often incorrectly called 'leaves'—there are no leaves), about 3–5 cm. ($1\frac{1}{4}$–2 in.) long and 1·5–2 cm. ($\frac{5}{8}$–$\frac{3}{4}$ in.) broad. The segments are rounded at the ends in the case of most of the usual hybrids, unlike the toothed segments of *Schlumbergera truncata*. These segments are joined end to end to produce long stems, and old specimens can make very large plants. The lower segments become woody, but the new growth should be a bright glossy green. It is not a difficult plant to cultivate, and magnificent specimens are sometimes seen, covered with bloom. Most of the troubles that do arise are due to errors of cultivation and can be overcome by attention to a few points. Occasionally one comes across the odd plant that will not succeed, and this may be due to a 'rogue' hybrid. If so, it is better to discard and try with another specimen.

New growth commences about May and continues until September, when the buds should start to form, on the ends of the terminal segments. The flowers open from about October until January or February, depending upon the variety and the conditions. The flowering time is influenced by the temperature of the room or greenhouse and the duration of light. 'Short day' treatment will tend to cause the buds to develop earlier, and too great a 'day' length (as can happen if the plants are exposed to long periods of artificial light) can inhibit flowering.

When the buds appear, the plants can be given a fortnightly feed with a liquid fertiliser, but this must be low in nitrogen and high in potassium, such as is given to tomatoes. Plants normally kept in a greenhouse can be brought indoors in the late autumn, when the extra warmth will help bud formation, but they should not be moved when in bud, or the buds drop. They can be returned to the cooler conditions after flowering. The flowers are about 5 cm. (2 in.) long, of a cerise colour, and more or less zygomorphic. They are scentless, but last for several days. The whole plant may be in bloom for several weeks.

After flowering, Christmas Cacti should be rested slightly until about May, when the new growth starts. They should, however, be given enough water to keep the compost slightly moist, and never allowed to dry out completely. During the rest of the year they should be watered freely. Plants kept indoors benefit from an occasional spraying. It is often an advantage to keep the plants out of doors in a semi-shady position during summer, but do not forget the watering.

Some growers experience trouble with bud dropping. This is usually due to sudden changes of temperature or draughty conditions, allowing the plant to become too dry, or changing its position relative to the direction of light.

The Christmas Cactus is not very particular about its compost.

Parodia faustiana

Rebutia minuscula forma *violaciflora*

Rebutia senilis

Sulcorebutia kruegeri. A grafted plant

Ariocarpus agavoides. An imported plant in a 5 cm. (2 in.) pot

Ariocarpus trigonus. An imported plant 10 cm. (4 in.) across

Encephalocarpus strobiliformis

*Epithelantha
micromeris*

*Lophophora
williamsii*

Utahia
sileri

Pediocactus
simpsonii

Pelecyphora aselliformis.
An old imported plant

Porfiria schwartzii. A
recently imported plant

*Sclerocactus
polyancistrus*

*Strombocactus
disciformis.* An
imported plant in
cultivation for
about 15 years

Uebelmannia pectinifera

Epiphyllum 'Cooperi'. A basal-flowering hybrid

Hatiora salicornioides

Rhipsalidopsis rosea

Rhipsalidopsis 'Paleface'. A spring-flowering hybrid

*Acanthorhipsalis
monacantha*

Schlumbergera
'Buckleyi'
(Christmas cactus)

Aporocactus flagelliformis

Heliocereus speciosus var. *albiflorus*

Cereus peruvianus monstrosus. Raised by the authors from a packet of cereus seed

Mammillaria discolor cristata

Lophophora williamsii cristata. A very large specimen

Epiphytes and other Large-flowered Cacti

It is important that the soil be well-drained and not become waterlogged. Pots should be large enough for the plant, but over-size pots should be avoided. If the stems become limp and dull-looking, the trouble probably lies with the soil or root conditions, and the cactus should be repotted. Too much sun may cause reddening of the stems—semi-shade is best.

Cuttings can be taken easily, pieces of stem of 2–3 segments are removed, allowed to dry off for a day or two and then potted up in the usual compost. The best time is spring and summer, but any other time is possible if some extra heat can be given.

The Christmas Cactus is self-sterile so that seeds will not be produced unless pollinated from a specimen of another variety.

A number of varieties of this popular plant have been produced by crossing between hybrids and back-crossing to the parents. Some of them have been given cultivar names and the reader may come across them. Probably the earliest to flower and one of the best is 'Konigers Weihnachtsfreude'. This is almost pure *Schlumbergera truncata* stock and has definite teeth to the stem segments and strongly zygomorphic flowers. These are orange-red in colour with a deeper throat. It is a vigorous and free-blooming plant, producing its first flowers well before Christmas, usually about November. Other hybrids, flowering around December, are 'Ballet Girl', 'Christmas Cheer', 'Orange Pippin', and 'Mr Thomas'. 'Grinda', in our experience, comes into flower rather later, about January. But the flowering times of these plants are quite variable, depending on environmental conditions, such as day length, as mentioned earlier.

A few of these hybrid cacti make an attractive addition to a collection. Since they can be grown at their best in hanging baskets, they can be suspended from the cross bars of a greenhouse, and do not take up too much room. If this position is too sunny, and the greenhouse is all-glass they can be suspended under the staging.

One newcomer to the genus *Schlumbergera* that we must mention here is *S. opuntioides*, formerly *Epiphyllanthus opuntioides*. Hunt has now included it in *Schlumbergera*. It is rather an unusual plant, very similar to a miniature opuntia, with areoles scattered over the flattened stem segments, but without glochids. There are small, spreading spines. The flowers, however, are typical schlumbergera, being very much like those of the Christmas Cactus, but a little more pinkish in colour. It is not an easy plant to grow and is probably better grafted.

Wittia

Borg mentions 2 species, *W. amazonica*, from Peru, and *W. panamensis*, from Panama and Columbia. These are similar to an epiphyllum, with long, hanging, leaf-like branches. The small red flowers are bell-shaped.

Zygocactus

This genus, originally including the well-known Christmas Cactus, is now considered to be congenic with *Schlumbergera*.

OTHER LARGE-FLOWERED CACTI

The epiphytic plants we have mentioned above belong to the so-called epiphylloid and rhipsaloid groups, and may be considered to be true epiphytes. There are, however, other large-flowered cacti, some of which are of a similar habit of growth, and this is a convenient place to consider them. Many of the plants belong to the cereoid group, and are climbers, attaching themselves by means of aerial roots to trees and bushes. Some are as epiphytic as any in the previous section, but they mostly differ in appearance from the epiphyllum and rhipsalis types already discussed.

As far as the cultivation of these plants is concerned, many of them can be grown under the same conditions as most of the cacti, and using the same composts. A few, however, prefer warmer conditions, and the richer composts of the epiphyllums. Unless otherwise stated, the plants in this section can be treated as suggested in the chapter on general cultivation.

Epiphytes and other Large-flowered Cacti

Acanthocereus

These are much-branched, shrubby cacti. The slender stems are usually erect at first and later spreading. They have 3 or more angles or ribs. The greenish-white, nocturnal flowers are large with a long tube. About 12 species have been described.

A. baxaniensis, from Mexico and Cuba, has stems about 4 cm. (1¾ in.) thick, and usually with 4 broad ribs. There are 5 or more brown radial spines 1·5 cm. (¾ in.) long and 1–3 thick centrals up to 3 cm. (1¼ in.) long. The flowers are freely produced and about 20 cm. (8 in.) in length.

A. brasiliensis comes from Brazil. The stems are weak, becoming sprawling or prostrate, up to 5 cm. (2 in.) thick and branching from the base. There are many needle-like spines, up to 2 cm. (¾ in.) long, radials and centrals similar. The flowers are up to 15 cm. (6 in.) long.

Aporocactus

A few species have been described, coming from Mexico and Central America, where they hang from trees or rocks.

A. flagelliformis is by far the best-known member of this genus. It is commonly called the 'Rat's-tail Cactus', due to its long, slender hanging stems, but it would be a large rat to have such a tail! It has been in cultivation for so long that its exact origin was uncertain until rediscovered in Mexico. The stems are up to 2 m. (6½ ft.) long and 1–1·5 cm. (around ½ in.) thick. They are closely ribbed and densely covered with small brownish spines. The cerise, tubular flowers are about 5 cm. (2 in.) across and are produced along the hanging stems in early spring. They last for several days. This cactus makes an ideal plant for hanging baskets, and seems to thrive in living-rooms. It does, however, require plenty of light, and will tolerate full sun, but complete dryness at the roots should be avoided, even in winter. In summer plenty of water should be given. The usual cactus compost is quite suitable.

A. flagriformis is far less common. The plant is similar to the above, but the stems are thicker and with fewer ribs.

A plant quite common in collections is often known as 'Aporocactus mallisonii'. This is, however, a misclassification as this cactus is a hybrid, correctly described as × *Heliaporus smithii*. It was first described in 1833, having been raised by Mallison as a cross between *A. flagelliformis* and *Heliocereus speciosus* (one of the parents of the epiphyllum hybrids). The female (seed) parent was the heliocereus, which the hybrid resembles in its stout stems and large red flowers, with a bluish flush inside. Since the stems eventually bend over, it makes as good a hanging basket plant as its aporocactus parent. It should be grown in full sun and watered freely in summer. Only frost protection is needed in winter. Cuttings root easily.

Other aporocactus species described include *A. martianus* and *A. conzattii*, of similar form to *A. flagelliformis*.

Cryptocereus

C. anthonyanus was discovered in 1946 in the forest of Ocozo-coautla in Chiapas, Mexico, and first bloomed in cultivation with Dr H. E. Anthony in 1950. The plant was at first thought to be a new species of *Epiphyllum* in the *anguiliger* group, but the stems are thicker and the plant has a climbing habit. It appears to be a 'missing link' between *Hylocereanae* and *Epiphyllanae*.

The climbing stems may reach a length of over 6 m. (20 ft.) and the branches are in clusters along the stems. These branches may be 1 m. (39 in.) or more in length and 7–15 cm. (2¾–6 in.) wide and deeply lobed. The areoles carry 3 small spines. The nocturnal flowers are about 12 cm. (4¾ in.) wide and fragrant. The outer petals are of a purplish colour and the inner cream.

The relationship of this cactus is rather obscure, but the flower is hylocereoid in type and the plant has been placed in the *Hylocereanae* group next to *Strophocactus*.

Deamia

This is a monotypic genus established for the unusual plant, *Deamia testudo*. The stems are of a variable shape, up to 25 cm. (10 in.) long, with aerial roots. They are flattened on the underside and produce adventitious roots, by means of which they cling to rocks and trees. The joints are strongly armed with long, dark spines. The white flowers may reach a diameter of 25 cm. (10 in.). This cactus comes from Honduras and requires full sun, warmth and a moist atmosphere.

Eriocereus and Harrisia

These two genera may be considered together as the names are often confused. Borg lists them all under *Harrisia*, but now around 8 species of *Eriocereus* and 13 of *Harrisia* are recognised, although some botanists prefer to lump them as *Eriocereus*. The distinction between the two genera is related to the seed-pods. In the case of the eriocerei the pods are red or carmine and usually burst to expose the seeds. The harrisias, on the other hand, have yellow or orange pods which do not split.

They are tall, slender cacti, and although the stems are at first erect, they soon become sprawling and need support in cultivation. There are usually several broad ribs, with spines. The flowers are large, usually white and nocturnal, often beginning to open in the early evening and remaining until the morning sunlight becomes strong. Although these cacti are large-growing, they grow upwards rather than outwards and the long stems can be trained up the side of a greenhouse and along the roof. They make useful grafting stock. The long stems are cut into pieces 5–8 cm. (2–3 in.) long, and rooted in the usual way.

Eriocerei are native to the mainland of South America and require the usual cactus treatment, but harrisias come from the West Indies and benefit from being kept warmer in winter.
Eriocereus bonplandii comes from Argentina, Brazil and Uruguay. The stems are up to about 3 m. (10 ft.) long in their native state and 3–6 cm. ($1\frac{1}{4}$–$2\frac{1}{4}$ in.) thick, and the areoles bear short spines. The flowers can reach 25 cm. (10 in.) long; they are white outside and greenish-brown inside. An 'Epiphyllum-type' compost is not necessary, the ordinary cactus compost being more suitable, or growth may be too lush at the expense of bloom.
E. jusbertii is very similar to the above plant. It is particularly valued as a grafting stock.
E. martinii, from Argentina, has rather thinner branches, almost cylindrical in shape, but with definite tubercles. These carry aeroles with greyish wool, a few short radial spines and one long

central. It is a particularly vigorous plant, much used for grafting. The white flowers are about 20 cm. (8 in.) long.

E. tortuosus has stems up to about 1 m. (39 in.) long, bearing spreading radial spines and stout centrals. The flowers are borne freely and the plant blooms freely when quite small.

Amongst the *Harrisia* we may mention *H. eriophora, H. gracilis* and *H. simpsonii*, although these are less often found in collections than *Eriocereus*.

Heliocereus

Heliocereus speciosus has been mentioned earlier as one of the parents of the many hybrid epicacti, although it is a terrestrial species. The stems are usually 4-angled and branch freely; they may reach up to 1 m. (39 in.) in length in nature. The areoles bear 5–8 brownish spines, about 1 cm. (⅜ in.) long. The diurnal flowers are truly beautiful, about 8–10 cm. (4–5 in.) across and of a brilliant carmine colour, with a purplish sheen. A rich soil is appreciated, but more sunlight can be given in summer than for the epiphyllums. This cactus comes from central Mexico.

Variety *albiflorus* (syn. *H. amecamensis*) is from Amecameca, Mexico. This is similar to the species, but the flowers are pure white.

A few other species of heliocereus are described, but are uncommon. Another red-flowered species is *H. cinnabarinus*.

Hylocereus

These are epiphytic or semi-epiphytic cacti. Their long climbing stems carry aerial roots by means of which they are attached to trees or rocks. The spines are either absent or very small and the large white flowers are nocturnal. About 18 species are described, all coming from the warm forest regions of Central America, Mexico and the West Indies. *Hylocereus* means 'wood-cereus', referring to the native forest or woody habitat. In cultivation the epiphytic conditions are suitable, but if possible, more warmth should be given in winter.

H. undatus is the best-known species, sometimes incorrectly called *Cereus triangularis*. The branched stems may grow to several metres in length, and up to 5 cm. (2 in.) diameter. They consist of large, deep green triangular joints. The spines are short and thick. The immense buds are followed by flowers up to 30 cm. (1 ft.) long. The red oval fruit is about 10 cm. (4 in.) long and is said to be edible and of good flavour.

Other species are far less common in cultivation but are similar in habit.

Mediocactus

These are mostly epiphytic plants, rather similar to *Heliocereus* in appearance, but with large, white nocturnal flowers, up to 25 cm. (10 in.) long. The spines are short.

M. setaceus from Brazil and Argentina has mostly erect, freely branching stems, and *M. megalanthus*, from Peru, has thinner hanging branches.

Monvillea

These are cacti with long, slender, rather prostrate stems and nocturnal flowers. They mostly come from Argentina, Brazil, and Paraguay. About 12 species have been described. They are quite easy in cultivation, grow rapidly, and will stand full sun.

M. cavendishii is the most usual species found in collections. The stems are about 1 m. (39 in.) long and 2 cm. ($\frac{3}{4}$ in.) thick. There are 9–10 rounded ribs and the areoles carry short spines. The white flowers are about 10 cm. (4 in.) across.

M. spegazzinii is of about the same size but with fewer ribs. It flowers particularly freely in early summer.

Nyctocereus

N. serpentinus is the only one of the few described species in general cultivation. It is a native of Mexico. The unjointed stems can reach several metres in length, and are about 2·5 cm. (1 in.) thick. There are about 12 ribs with spines up to about 1 cm. ($\frac{3}{8}$ in.) long. The nocturnal flowers are about 15 cm. (6 in.) across; they are white and scented. The plant grows vigorously, and the long stems may be cut into sections, rooted and used as grafting stock.

Epiphytes and other Large-flowered Cacti

Peniocereus

P. greggii, or the 'Arizona Queen of the Night', is one of the most beautiful of the night-blooming cacti, but rather difficult in cultivation. It consists of a long turnip-like root, which serves for water storage, and stems up to 3 m. (10 ft.) long and 2 cm. ($\frac{3}{4}$ in.) thick. The rootstock may weigh as much as 50 kg. (1 cwt.). The flowers, opening in the evening, are pure white and strongly perfumed. They are about 15–20 cm. (6–8 in.) long. Cultivated specimens must be watered very carefully, unless grafted. This cactus, as the name implies, is native to Arizona in North America, and extends its range into north Mexico.

The Zürich collection lists 4 other species, *P. fosterianus*, *P. maculatus, P. marnierianus,* and *P. rosea,* all from Mexico.

Selenicereus

This is another genus of long-stemmed, straggly cacti, including over 25 species, only 2 of which are at all well known. As in the case of *Nyctocereus*, portions of *Selenicereus* stem, when rooted, make excellent grafting stock.

S. grandiflorus. Another 'Queen of the Night', this time coming from the West Indies. The trailing or climbing stems are 2–3 cm. (1 in.–1$\frac{1}{4}$ in.) thick and up to 5 m. (16 ft.) in length, although cultivated specimens are likely to be smaller. They are greyish-green in colour with 5–7 ribs, and short needle-like spines. The immense, nocturnal, white flowers are strongly scented with a vanilla-like perfume. They are about 30 cm. (1 ft.) long and bell-shaped.

S. macdonaldiae comes from Argentina and Uruguay. The stem is a dark glossy green, otherwise the plant is similar to the preceding, except that the flowers are almost scentless.

Strophocactus

A monotypic genus, consisting of a little-known plant, *S. wittii,* worthy of mention because it is unusual and the reader may possibly come across a reference to it. The type species was found in swampy forests near Manaos, Upper Amazon, in Brazil, although a specimen in this country apparently does not necessarily like swampy conditions and appreciates sun. The flattened stem is about 7 cm. (2¾ in.) wide with spines along the edges. It twines around the trunks and branches of trees, gripping by means of aerial roots, much as with our ivy. It was originally considered to be related to the epiphyllums, but was later realised to be of the *Cereus* type, akin to *Selenicereus*. The flowers are said to be reddish, about 25 cm. (10 in.) long.

Weberocereus

These are rare epiphytic plants from Central America. They have long, slender, trailing stems, flat or 3-angled, and with small spines. The nocturnal flowers are smaller than most of those in this section, being 5 cm. (2 in.) long and white or pink in colour. Borg mentions 3 species, *W. biolleyi, W. panamensis* and *W. tumilla.* Anyone who tries to cultivate these cacti should give them a winter temperature of about 10 °C (50 °F).

Werkleocereus

More rare epiphytic cacti from Central America where they are found in warm, moist forests. They are trailing in habit, with slender, jointed triangular stems, and aerial roots. The pink or yellow flowers are about 8 cm. (3 in.) long. Borg describes 2 species, *W. tonduzii* and *W. glaber.* Warmer conditions are needed.

Wilcoxia

These cacti have tuberous roots and slender, weak stems. The diurnal flowers are purplish-red and about 5 cm. (2 in.) long. They last for several days. Like all tuberous-rooted cacti, it is necessary to have a pot sufficiently large to contain the tuber, or growth will be stunted. However, *Wilcoxia* are often grown grafted. 5 species are described, only 2 of which are at all common.

W. poselgeri from south Texas and Mexico, has stems 30–60 cm. (1–2 ft.) long and about 1 cm. (⅜ in.) thick. They are cylindrical with about 8 ribs and very small spines.

W. schmollii has rather shorter, thicker stems than the previous plant, and they are covered with silky, whitish hair.

Willmattea

This is a monotypic genus established to include the unusual species *W. minutiflora* (formerly *W. viridiflora*) a climbing epiphyte from the forests of Guatemala and Honduras. The slender stems are dark green and triangular, carrying small spines. The sweet scented, nocturnal flowers are about 5 cm. (2 in.) long. The plant is unlikely to be met in cultivation.

ELEVEN

Cristate and Monstrous Plants

These 'distorted' plants are very much an acquired taste. There are growers who specialise in 'crests', and there are other collectors who think that such monstrosities should be destroyed at birth! For ourselves, while we can see the beauty of other people's cristates, we have no great desire to fill our own greenhouses with expensive 'crests'.

Before discussing these plants further we must mention the term 'fasciation', which is a type of malformation on top of a plant; if it is symmetrical, it is popularly known as a 'crest'. A crest or cristate plant is caused by the growing tip becoming multiple and developing laterally, forming a flattened, ribbon-shaped growth. This eventually becomes twisted and convoluted. Sometimes multiple centres develop at the growing tip, producing a monstrous plant. These plants are covered with irregular, often knob-like, growths.

Fasciation is common amongst cacti, particularly the opuntias and mammillarias. Cristate forms have, however, been found in almost all genera. We have seen photographs of enormous specimens of *Carnegiea gigantea* which have produced one cristate branch. Amongst our own cacti, we have had plants which suddenly produced an odd-looking off-set or branch. But we have had very little success in establishing these deformed plants, either as grafts or on their own roots. Occasionally, a packet of seed will give rise to one or two oddities. These start off as normal seedlings and develop their fasciation later.

The process of fasciation has intrigued both growers and botanists for a long time. Once it was thought that crests were caused by physical damage to the growing tip. 'Unspeakable atrocities' were committed in the name of science; plants were attacked with everything from acids to knives. As far as we can discover, there has not been one single, permanent, man-made 'crest' as a result of all this activity. Fasciation may be a hereditary factor, although it may require a cultural shock to show its presence. It was at one time thought that cristate and monstrous plants did not flower. This has been disproved, although the flowers may be smaller than those of the normal plant. Anyone who has grown the very common *Mammillaria wildii cristata* will have had no trouble in flowering it.

Research on fasciation amongst the cacti has been done by G. D. Rowley. Altogether, he sowed 100 seeds of each of 11 species. He found that the percentage fasciation varied from 0 in *Cereus alacriportanus, C. dayamii* and *C. gonianthus,* to as high as 66·7 in *C. horribarbis.* He also sowed seed collected from *Cereus peruvianus monstrosus.* The young seedlings had a very high mortality rate, 40 per cent dying, and of the survivors 34·3 per cent were fasciated. Some of these were very dwarf specimens, even slower growing than the monstrous plants that occur occasionally from packets of 'normal' cereus seed. We have raised young plants of *C. peruvianus* and have now a couple of monstrous specimens that came up amongst the ordinary cerei. They are a fraction of the size of their relatives.

The most desirable and probably the most expensive monstrous cactus is *Lophocereus schottii monstrosus,* the 'Totem-pole' cactus. The ribs and spines have disappeared and the plant consists of green knobs and bumps which could almost have been carved. Howard Gates found a colony of these plants in one of the most arid regions of Baja California (monstrous and cristate plants do sometimes occur in groups). A surprising thing about them was that they showed no tendency to form normal shoots. Many fasciated cacti bear vigorous normal shoots which must be removed if they are not to swamp the abnormal part.

If some of our readers wish to add a few cristate and monstrous cacti to their collections without spending a fortune, the following plants are freely available: *Mammillaria discolor cristata, Mammillaria wildii cristata, Opuntia cylindrica cristata,* and *Opuntia vestita cristata.* Amongst the monstrous plants, *Cereus jamacaru* and *C. peruvianus* both have common monstrous forms. In fact if a packet of seed of these species is bought, it is more than likely that at least one monstrous seedling will appear. There is also *Opuntia tuna monstrosa*. Most monstrous plants are grown on their own roots whilst, with the exception of *Mammillaria wildii cristata*, cristates are usually grown grafted. However, in the wild they survive on their own roots, and judging from some of the large imports we have seen, they live for a long time without any assistance from the grafting knife.

GLOSSARY

Some of these terms have been explained in the text, but we feel that it is convenient to group them together in a short glossary, and to give further explanation where needed.

Actinomorphic A flower which is radially symmetrical or REGULAR (cf.).

Areole A specific organ found only in the cactus family. It is a cushion-like structure, representing a telescoped lateral branch. The spines, flowers and off-sets arise from this organ.

Caespitose Clump-forming with off-sets produced from around the base.

Callus The hardened tissue forming over the cut portion of a cactus.

Calyx The outer floral envelope.

Cephalium A woolly swelling at the top and sometimes the side of certain cacti in which the buds are formed. The cephalium increases in size with age.

Chlorophyll The green pigment in plants, essential for the manufacture of food.

Chlorotic Having a yellow appearance from insufficient chlorophyll. The condition is usually due to conditions of poor light, although some abnormal cacti have no chlorophyll.

Cleistogomous Having flowers which self pollinate without opening.

191

Glossary

Clone A group of plants all produced from one parent by vegetative propagation.

Corolla The part of the flower between the calyx and the stamens; the collective term for petals.

Cotyledon The first leaf or leaf pair emerging from the seed.

Cristate Having fasciated growth of fan-like form. (cf. MONSTROUS)

Dichotomous Branching by forking into two equal parts.

Diurnal When applied to flowers, it means opening during the hours of daylight, and closing at night. (cf. NOCTURNAL)

Epidermis The skin or outermost layer of cells of a plant, below the cuticle.

Epiphyte A plant which grows on another plant, using it as a support only. It obtains no water or nourishment from the supporting plant.

Etiolated Having a pale colour and long, straggly growth, caused by lack of light.

Family A division of plants made up of genera.

Fasciated An abnormal growth on a plant due to disorganisation of the growing point.

Genus (Plural **Genera**) A taxonomic unit made up of allied species.

Monotypic Said of a genus containing only a single species.

Monstrous Showing a type of fasciation with a many-centred growing point. (cf. CRISTATE)

Nocturnal Applied to flowers opening during the hours of darkness. (cf. DIURNAL)

Peduncle The stalk or stem of a flower, or the main stem of an inflorescence.

Perianth The collective term for petals and sepals.

Glossary

Petal   The (usually) coloured part of the flower which is inside the sepals. See COROLLA

Photosynthesis   The process by which carbon dioxide and water are converted into carbohydrates, the energy for this being supplied by sunlight.

Polymorphic   Existing in many forms.

Pseudocephalium   A hairy growth formed when normal areoles start developing long hairs so that a head superficially resembling a true cephalium is formed.

Regular   Applied to a flower when the corolla is made up of similarly shaped petals equally spaced; it is radially symmetrical or ACTINOMORPHIC (cf.).

Scion   In a graft, the scion is the unrooted section of stem attached to the stock.

Self-fertile   Capable of setting seed with its own pollen.

Self-sterile   Incapable of setting seed with its own pollen.

Sepal   The outermost flower structures which form the calyx.

Solitary   Unbranched and without off-sets.

Species   A group of closely similar plants, breeding amongst themselves. Species are grouped to form genera.

Stock   In a graft, the stock is the rooted section of stem.

Stigma   The expanded top of the style to which the pollen adheres.

Style   The narrow column joining the stigma to the ovary.

Succulent   A plant which is able to store water in its tissues enabling it to survive periods of drought.

Taxonomist   A specialist in classification.

Tubercle   A protuberance on the stems of certain cacti, mainly mammillarias, on the tips of which are situated the areoles.

Glossary

Type Species   The species whose characteristics were first described and on which the genus is based. These plants are usually deposited in herbaria.

Xerophyte   A drought-resistant plant; not necessarily succulent.

Zygomorphic   Opposite to REGULAR or ACTINOMORPHIC applied to flowers. The flower can be divided into two halves in one plane only. It is bilaterally symmetrical.

BIBLIOGRAPHY

The following are some of the standard works on the *Cactaceae*:

Curt Backeberg	*Das Kakteenlexikon*
„	*Die Cactaceae* (6 vol.)
Lyman Benson	*The Cacti of Arizona* (University of New Mexico Press, 1950)
„	*The Native Cacti of California* (Stanford University Press, 1969)
J. Borg	*Cacti* (London: Blandford Press)
N. L. Britton and J. N. Rose	*Cactaceae* (New York: Dover)
Franz Buxbaum	*Cactus Culture based on Biology* (London: Blandford Press)
Claude Chidamian	*Book of Cacti and Other Succulents* (New York: Doubleday)
R. T. Craig	*The Mammillaria Handbook* (New York: Johnson Reprint Corp.)
Zürich Collection Catalogue	German text, but lists of Latin plant names Useful only for nomenclature

GENERAL INDEX

Page numbers in italics indicate a plate facing or following page number given

Areole, 17, 19

Bonemeal, 32
Bowl gardens, 37, *48*

Cactaceae, characteristics of, 17
Cacti, cristate, 187–89
  desert, 19, *48*
  monstrous, 187–89
Cholla, 54–5
Classification, 27–9
Compost, for epiphytes, 30, 178
  moss on surface of, 45
  no-soil, 31, 42
Cross-pollination, 21
Cuttings, 47–48
  callusing, 48
  time to take, 48

Deficiency, nutrient, 41
Desert, 22
Diseases, 41
Disorders, physiological, 41
Drainage, 30, 31, 41

Epiphytes, 19, 23, 24, 35, 36, 164–86

Fasciation, 187–89
Fertilisers, 32
Flower, 20
Flowering time, 24
Fungus gnat *see* sciarid fly

Glochid, 19
Grafting, 48–50, *48*

Habitat, 22–4
Hair, 19

Heating, methods of, 36–7
Hybrid, 21

Leaf, 18

Malathion, damage to plants, 39
Mealy bug, 39, *48*
  root, 39–40
Moisture, 43, 44, 45
Mushroom fly *see* sciarid fly
Myths, 24

Nomenclature, 26–9

Off-sets, 47
Opuntias, hardy, 60
Overwintering, 33–4

Pests, 39–40
Pots, clay, 30–1
  plastic, 30–1
Plant, succulent, 17–18

Red spider mite, 40
Repotting, 30–2
Roots, 18–19
Rot, 41

Scale insects, 40
Sciarid fly, 40
Seed, 42–6, 58, 92, *48*
  compost, 42, 43
  freshness, 42–3
  method of sowing, 44
  pricking out, 45–6
  ripeness, 46, 92
  shade, 45
  temperature, 43
  tephrocacti, 58

INDEX OF PLANTS

Page numbers in italics indicate a plate facing or following page number given

Index of Plants

Index of Plants

Index of Plants

Index of Plants

Index of Plants

Index of Plants